T0360463

Rethinking Culture, Organization and Management

The purpose of this book is to reimagine the concept of culture, both as an analytical category and disciplinary practice of dominance, marginalization and exclusion. For decades culture has been perceived as a 'hot topic'. It has been written about and deployed as part of 'a search for excellence'; as a tool through which to categorise, rank, motivate and mould individuals; as a part of an attempt to align individual and corporate goals; as a driver of organizational change, and; as a servant of profit maximisation. The women writers presented in this book offer a different take on culture: they offer useful disruptions to mainstream conceptions of culture. Joanne Martin and Mary Douglas provide multi-dimensional holistic accounts of social relations that point up similarity and difference. Rather than offering totalising or prescriptive models, each author considers the complex, polyphonic and processual nature of culture(s) while challenging us to acknowledge and work with ambiguity, fluidity and disruption. In this spirit writings of Judi Marshall, Arlie Hochschild, Kathy Ferguson, Luce Irigaray and Donna Haraway are employed to disrupt extant management cultures that lionise the masculine and marginalise the concerns, perspectives and contributions of women and the diversity of women. These writers bring bodies, emotions, difference, resistance and politics back to the centre stage of organizational theory and practice. They open us up to the possibility of cultures suffused with multifarious potentiality rather than homogeneity and faux certainty. As such, they offer new ways of understanding and performing culture in management and organization.

This book will be relevant to students and researchers across business and management, organizational studies, critical management studies, gender studies and sociology.

Robert McMurray is Professor of Work and Organization at The York Management School, UK.

Alison Pullen is Professor of Management and Organization Studies at Macquarie Business School, Sydney, Australia.

Routledge Focus on Women Writers in Organization Studies

Given that women and men have always engaged in and thought about organizing, why is it that core management texts are dominated by the writing of men? This series redresses the neglect of women in organization thought and practice and highlights their contributions. Through a selection of carefully curated short-form books, it covers major themes such as structure, rationality, managing, leading, culture, power, ethics, diversity and sustainability; and also attends to contemporary debates surrounding performativity, the body, emotion, materiality and post-coloniality. Individually, each book provides stand-alone coverage of a key sub-area within organization studies, with a contextual series introduction written by the editors. Collectively, the titles in the series give a global overview of how women have shaped organizational thought.

Routledge Focus on Women Writers in Organization Studies will be relevant to students and researchers across business and management, organizational studies, critical management studies, gender studies and sociology.

Beyond Rationality in Organization and Management
Edited by Robert McMurray and Alison Pullen

Power, Politics and Exclusion in Organization and Management
Edited by Robert McMurray and Alison Pullen

Gender, Embodiment and Fluidity in Organization and Management
Edited by Robert McMurray and Alison Pullen

Rethinking Culture, Organization and Management
Edited by Robert McMurray and Alison Pullen

Morality, Ethics and Responsibility in Organization and Management
Edited by Robert McMurray and Alison Pullen

For more information about this series, please visit: www.routledge.com/ Routledge-Focus-on-Women-Writers-in-Organization-Studies/book-series/ RFWWOS

Rethinking Culture, Organization and Management

Edited by Robert McMurray and Alison Pullen

Routledge
Taylor & Francis Group

LONDON AND NEW YORK

First published 2020
by Routledge
2 Park Square, Milton Park, Abingdon, Oxon OX14 4RN

and by Routledge
52 Vanderbilt Avenue, New York, NY 10017

Routledge is an imprint of the Taylor & Francis Group, an informa business

© 2020 selection and editorial matter, Robert McMurray and Alison Pullen; individual chapters, the contributors

The right of Robert McMurray and Alison Pullen to be identified as the authors of the editorial material, and of the authors for their individual chapters, has been asserted in accordance with sections 77 and 78 of the Copyright, Designs and Patents Act 1988.

British Library Cataloguing-in-Publication Data
A catalogue record for this book is available from the British Library

Library of Congress Cataloging-in-Publication Data
A catalog record has been requested for this book

ISBN: 978-0-367-23410-2 (hbk)
ISBN: 978-0-429-27972-0 (ebk)

Typeset in Times New Roman
by Deanta Global Publishing Services, Chennai, India

Contents

Series note

This series arose from the question: given that women and men have always engaged in, and thought about, organizing, why are core management texts dominated by the writing of men? Relatedly, and centrally to the development of organization studies as a field, the following questions rose: Why do so few women theorists and writers appear in our lectures and classes on managing, organizing and working? Why has the contribution of women to organization theory been neglected, indeed, written out of, the everyday conversations of the academy?

This series redresses the neglect of women in organization thought and practice. It does so by highlighting the unique contributions of women in respect to fundamental organizational issues such as structure, rationality, managing, leading, culture, power, ethics, diversity and sustainability, while also attending to more nuanced organizational concerns arising from issues such as performativity, the body, emotion, materiality and post-coloniality.

Through a selection of carefully curated short-form books, the series provides an overview of how women have shaped organizational thought. This series is international in scope, drawing on ideas, concepts, experiences and writing from across Europe, North America, Australasia and spanning more than 150 years. As the series develops our ambition is to move beyond even these confines to encompass the work of women from all parts of the globe.

This is not a standard textbook. It does not offer a chronological history of women in organization theory. It does not (cannot) claim to be the complete or the last word on women in organization: the contribution of women to organization theory and practice continues and grows. We do not even promise that each chapter will be written like the one that preceded it! Why? It is because the variation in style and substance of each chapter deliberately reflects the varied, exciting and often transgressive women discussed. Indeed, one of the points of this series is to draw attention to the possibility that there are as many ways of thinking about, writing on and doing organizing as there are people. If you want to read and think differently about management, work and organization then this is the series for you.

Readers of this and other volumes in the series will note that the first person is often employed in our accounts of women writers. Reference is made to meetings with writers, to the personal impact of their thinking, and the ways in which writers have moved or challenged their researches personally. Once again, this personal emotional approach to assessing the work of others is at with odds with more positivistic or masculine approaches that contend that the researcher or analyst of organizations is to remain outside, beyond or above the subject matter: an expert eye whose authorial tone allows them to act as dispassionate judge on the work of others. We argue that the fallacy of neutrality that results from such masculine positivism hides the arbitrary and inherently biased nature of subject selection, appraisal and writing. Just as importantly, it tends to produce sterile prose that does little to convey the excitement and dynamism of the ideas being discussed.

The subject matter of this book has been chosen because the chapter creators believe them to be important, and thought has been given to the selection of the women writers shared with you. Authors recognise the bias inherent in any writing project; it is writ-large in the title (*Focus on Women Writers*) and is more explicit in some chapters than others. In editing this series, we have been struck with the enthusiasm that informs how our authors have chosen influential women writers, and this enthusiasm can be read in the ways in which the chapters engage with the work of specific writers, the application of these writers to organization studies and the personal reflections of the influence of writers on their own research. The perspective from which we – and our authors – write is therefore open for you (the reader) to read, acknowledge and account for in the multiple ways intended. The lack of consistency with which the authors address fundamental organizational issues should not be read as lacking rigour, but rather bring an alternative way of leveraging critical thinking through an engaged, personal approach to the field. In this way, authors embody the ideas and ethos of the women writers chosen. While written in an accessible form, each chapter is based on years of engagement with the works of women writers and an in-depth appreciation of their contribution to and impact on organization studies. There is also critique. The omissions or controversies that have accompanied the work of these writers is addressed, along with challenges to their work.

The result is a collection of books on *Women Writers* that are scholarly, readable and engaging. They introduce you to some of the most important concepts in organization studies and from some of the best theorists in the field. Politically and ethically we hope that this book will help students, lecturers and practitioners reverse a trend that has seen women writers written-out of organization theory. Just as importantly, the inclusion of such work usefully challenges many long-held beliefs within mainstream management literature. We hope that this series will be the beginning of your own personal journey of ideas – the text and suggested readings produced in this book offering starting point for your own discoveries.

Routledge Focus on Women Writers in Organization Studies will be relevant to students, teachers and researchers across business and management, organizational studies, critical management studies, gender studies and sociology.

Contributors

Lotte Holck is Associate Professor at the Department of Organization, Copenhagen Business School. Holck's research is on the organization of work and collaboration in different organizational settings and cultural contexts. Her main research interests include management and development of human resources (HRM), organizational inequality, diversity and inclusion, and bodies and embodiment in organizations. Holck applies longitudinal ethnographic studies using qualitative methodologies of participatory observations, interviews and interventions. Her work has appeared in journals such as *Organization, Scandinavian Journal of Management, Personnel Review, Qualitative Research in Organizations and Management: An International Journal* and *Equality, Diversity and Inclusion: An International Journal.*

Department of Organization, Copenhagen Business School, Denmark.
lho.ioa@cbs.dk

Jason Hughes is Professor and Head of Media, Communication and Sociology at the University of Leicester, UK. His research interests include problematised consumption, drugs, addiction and health; emotions work and identity; figurational sociology and sociological theory; moral panics and regulation. Recent authored/co-authored and co-edited books have focussed on the sociology of Norbert Elias, visual methods and archival research.

School of Media, Communication and Sociology,
University of Leicester, UK.
jason.hughes@le.ac.uk

Robert McMurray is Professor of Work and Organization at The York Management School, UK. Research interests include the organization of health care, professions, emotion labour, dirty work and visual methods. Other collaborative book projects include *The Dark Side of Emotional Labour* (2015, Routledge), *The Management of Wicked Problems in Health and Social Care* (2018, Routledge) and *Urban Portraits* (2017, Coffee Stop Publishing).

The York Management School, University of York, UK.
Robert.mcmurray@york.ac.uk

Sara L. Muhr is Professor at Copenhagen Business School. She is also Academic Director of the CBS Business in Society Platform 'Diversity and Difference'. Her research focuses on critical perspectives on managerial identity and HRM, especially in relation to issues around coping with diversity and expectations in modern, flexible ways of working. Following this broader aim, she has worked in various empirical settings such as management consultancy, prisons, the military and police force, pole dancing studios and executive networks where she has engaged with issues such as power, culture, emotional labour, gender, ethnicity, migration, leadership and work-life balance.

Department of Organization, Copenhagen Business School, Denmark.
slm.ioa@cbs.dk

Ajnesh Prasad is the Canada Research Chair in the School of Business at Royal Roads University in Canada. His research interests broadly focus on entrepreneurship, gender and diversity issues in organizations, and interpretive methods. He earned his PhD in organization studies from York University's Schulich School of Business.

School of Business, Royal Roads University, Victoria, Canada.
ajnesh_prasad@yahoo.ca

Alison Pullen is Professor of Management and Organization Studies at Macquarie Business School, Sydney, Australia and Editor-in-Chief of *Gender, Work and Organization*. Alison's research has been concerned with analysing and intervening in the politics of work as it concerns gender discrimination, identity politics and organizational injustice.

Department of Management, Macquarie Business School, Sydney, Australia.
Alison.pullen@mq.edu.au

Paulina Segarra is Assistant Professor in the Faculty of Business and Economics at Anáhuac University in Mexico. Her research interests focus on the experiences of undocumented immigrants at work. She earned her PhD in management from Tecnologico de Monterrey's EGADE Business School.

Universidad Anáhuac México, Mexico.
paulina.segarra@gmail.com

Ruth Simpson is Professor of Management at Brunel Business School. Her research interests include gender and organizations; inequality and 'dirty work'; and gender and careers. She has authored, co-authored and co-edited several books including: *Dirty Work: Concepts and Identities* (2012); *The Handbook in Gender and Organizations* (2014); *Gender, Class and Occupation* (2016) and *Postfeminism and Organisation* (2017). She has had several editorial roles and has published in leading journals including *Human Relations, Organization, Work, Employment and Society, The Academy of Management (Learning and Education), Management Learning* and *Gender, Work and Organization*.

Brunel Business School, Brunel University, UK.
r.simpson@brunel.ac.uk

Amanda Sinclair is an author, researcher, teacher and consultant in leadership, change, gender and diversity. Currently a Professorial Fellow, Sinclair held the Foundation Chair of Management (Diversity and Change) at Melbourne Business School from 1995–2012. Her books include: *Doing Leadership Differently* (1998); *Leadership for the Disillusioned* (2007); *Leading Mindfully* (2016); and, with Christine Nixon, *Women Leading* (2017). Sinclair has coaching and consulting experience in corporate, medical, police, school, union, judicial, university and government settings. She is also a yoga and meditation teacher who seeks to support people towards sustainable ways of being in leadership.

Melbourne Business School, The University of Melbourne, Australia.
a.sinclair@mbs.edu

Sheena J. Vachhani is a Reader (Associate Professor) in Work and Organization Studies and Co-Director of the Centre for Action Research and Critical Inquiry in Organisations (ARCIO) at the School of Management, University of Bristol, UK. Her work centres on ethics, politics, and difference in work and organization. She is currently engaged in a number of research projects on these themes, including: feminist politics and activism using archival research; craft practices and new materialism; solidarity and vulnerability; and corporeality in physical labour under neoliberalism. She is an associate editor for *Gender, Work and Organization* and publishes in scholarly journals such as: *Human Relations, Organization Studies, Work, Employment and Society*, and *Organization*.

School of Management, University of Bristol, UK.
s.vachhani@bristol.ac.uk

Cristian E. Villanueva is Assistant Professor in the Faculty of Business and Economics at Anáhuac University in Mexico. His research interests focus on entrepreneurship. He earned his PhD in management from Tecnologico de Monterrey's EGADE Business School.

Universidad Anáhuac México, Mexico.
crisvaider@hotmail.com

1 Introduction

Rethinking culture, organization and management

Robert McMurray and Alison Pullen

As with the first three books of the **Focus on Women Writers in Organization Studies** series, this volume champions exemplary research and theorising that mainstream accounts have over-simplified or over-looked. The purpose of this book is to reimagine the concept of culture, both as an analytical category and a disciplinary practice of dominance, marginalization and exclusion. Women writers that have developed critical conceptualizations of culture have been employed to understand the ways in which culture creates and conditions power relations that perpetuate and reinforce the dominance of some bodies, at the expense and exclusion of other bodies (see books 2 and 3 in this series on power and embodiment).

For decades culture has been perceived as a 'hot topic'. In the 1980s culture was written about and deployed as part of 'a search for excellence' in organization and management. Culture has been used as tool through which to categorise, rank, motivate and mould individuals and groups to align corporate and organizational goals and to maximise effectiveness and profits. As management 'fad and fashion' culture has been engaged to drive organizational change through the alignment of vision, policies, rituals, story-telling and observable practice in the name of 'strong culture' and consensual top-down organizing. Where cultures are found to vary by nationality or geography they are to be mapped, understood and harnessed. In this way cultural difference can be shaped to generic organizational goals.

The writers presented in this book offer a different take on culture: they offer useful disruptions to mainstream conceptions of culture. The authors of our first two chapters present us with what most readers would recognise as models of culture that develop a critical reading of culture. Joanne Martin's 'Three Perspectives' and Mary Douglas's 'Grid-group cultural theory' set out to provide multi-dimensional holistic accounts of social relations that account for similarity and difference. Rather than offering totalising or prescriptive models, each author points to the complex, polyphonic and processual nature of culture(s). These writers challenge us to acknowledge and work with complexity, ambiguity, fluidity and disruption. That challenge is made real as each chapter moves from overt culture narratives to address cultures of sexism, injustice, otherness and inequality that are more subjective, invisible and less tangible. Rather than take for granted these critical accounts of culture, each author encourages the reader to embody a critical reading from our own individual perspective. We see how even critical accounts of management have ghettoised feminist theory, rendering it (in Douglas's terms) as 'dirt', dirt which disrupts and undoes norms. In relation to culture, cultural norms and normalised values of an organization can be disrupted by understanding the ambiguity of knowledge, differences of perspective and bodies, and changes over time.

Subsequent chapters take this critical challenge further as authors discuss the ways in which dominant masculine cultures enforce ways of working that threaten diversity of experience and bodies. They look at the ways in which discourses of neutrality and rationality such as gender-neutral accounts of organizations and management have ignored difference and suffocated feminist thought and experiences of marginalization. These writers provide alternative accounts of organizing and being which are central to understanding the cultural diversity of organizations and which are central to understanding 'the way we do things around here'. Such ideas foster an understanding of the differences between corporate culture as a management strategy and practice, and organizational culture as practices and processes created and maintained over time by the organization's members, whose bodies and experiences are different. These chapters champion the cultural importance of difference. The writings of Judi Marshall, Arlie Hochschild, Kathy Ferguson, Luce Irigaray and Donna Haraway are employed to disrupt extant management cultures that lionise the masculine and marginalise the concerns, perspectives, contributions and diversity of women. These writers bring bodies, emotions, difference, resistance and politics back to the centre stage of organizational theory and practice. They offer hope in the form of diversity of experience and bodies that disrupt normalised understandings of culture. They open us up to the possibility of cultures suffused with multifarious potentiality rather than homogeneity and faux certainty. As such, they offer new ways of understanding and performing culture in management and organization.

In Chapter 2, Lotte Holck and Sara Louise Muhr highlight the nuanced writing of **Joanne Martin** – a sociologist whose work on culture has been overlooked and under-utilised when compared to textbook staples such as Schein and Hofstede. Spanning social justice, feminist theory, research process and culture, Martin's work is presented as multi-dimensional and critical. Martin's most well-known work on culture posits that a holistic understanding of organizational culture must account for three inter-related perspectives, described as: integration, differentiation and fragmentation. Discussing these perspectives, the chapter illustrates the ways in which Joanne Martin challenges the reductionism and simplification that characterises extant theory and practice on culture in organizational contexts, while at the same time acknowledging the value that is to be found in both theory and practice. Martin calls on those who study organizational culture to embrace and account for ambiguity and fluidity as well as multiplicity in such a way that disrupts our fantasies of clean, rational, unitary and orderly organizing. We also learn that Martin's disruption of neat fantasies extends to challenging the culture of Critical Management Studies (CMS) for its relative neglect of gender, the discrimination inherent in the structures and processes of higher learning, and a deconstruction of 'founding fathers [sic]'.

The cultural significance of cleanliness, or more precisely dirt, lies at the heart of Chapter 3, in which Ruth Simpson and Jason Hughes introduce us to **Mary Douglas**, whose work is central to the field of anthropology and gaining traction in organizational studies. Douglas's work is shown to be wide-ranging in its scope and impact, traversing issues as diverse as culture, economics, terrorism, consumer choice, poverty, environmentalism and governance. Running through Douglas's work is a concern with how our perceptions and relations are informed by the social and institutional contexts in which we find ourselves. Douglas's work provides a framework for considering why people behave in certain ways by assessing the cultural forces that shape us. Labelled Grid-Group or Cultural Theory, this is perhaps the most well-known aspect of Douglas's work in organization studies. Ruth Simpson and Jason Hughes point out that within this work there is also a concern with dirt. Specifically, a consideration of dirt in symbolical and material terms is shown to increase our understanding of preferred or cherished ways of ordering and controlling the world around us. As Simpson and Hughes go on to discuss, this has given rise to a growing body of work that seeks to understand the nature and effects of dirty work in contemporary society and the practical and cultural imperatives that attend such tasks. In cultural terms Douglas's early work can be used to examine emerging cultural practices of 'ritual purity' in organizations and how they 'inflect' modern, contextually driven notions of conformity, morality and transgression. Ruth Simpson and Jason Hughes conclude that such an examination may encompass how appeals to, and images of, purity and impurity shape the organizational subject, as well as how they form the basis for organizational and wider discourses such as those around morality, inequality and fairness. Issues of inequality and its cultural roots and implications are writ large in the remaining chapters of this book.

In Chapter 4, Amanda Sinclair provides a highly original and personal reflexive account of the impact of three foundational feminist writers on her own research, practice and writing: **Judi Marshall, Arlie Hochschild and Kathy Ferguson**. We come to understand how, in the face of masculine disciplinary cultures that marginalise the concerns, lives and achievements of women, each writer disrupts extant management literature and more narrowly conceived assumptions on the nature of organizing. This is a deliberately personal account that challenges the abstractionism and faux neutrality of much management writing and reviewing to explain how the work of Marshall, Hochschild and Ferguson can change the course of a scholastic life and, with it, how we might reimagine the world around us. In so doing, Amanda Sinclair's own feminism challenges the dominant culture of organization studies for its marginalization of women, its lack of interdisciplinarity and lack of readability. Judi Marshall's work is highlighted as particularly instructive in this regard, providing as it does insight into the way women are encouraged to be invisible to self and other, particularly in the workplace. Cultures that lionise the masculine are shown to marginalise the concerns, perspectives and contributions of women. Further evidence is provided through reference to Hochschild's work on emotional labour and the power lines that position such forms of labour as women's work and, thus, as less valuable. Finally, the work of Kathy Ferguson is considered and the contention that bureaucratic hierarchies perpetuate cultures of suppression. All three writers provoke and transgress extant modes of thinking about organizing by bringing emotion, resistance, gender and politics centre stage to challenge masculine conceptions of discipline, leadership, organizing and privilege. Collective feminist thought is produced to effectively challenge discourses of neutrality that mask masculinity. In this sense they challenge a culture so dominant in organizational and managerial terms that it frequently goes unseen.

Many of the themes developed by Amanda Sinclair are pursued in Chapter 5 as Sheena J. Vachhani contemplates the place of the visceral, embodied, material, maternal, feminine and sexuate in organizational writing and practice, focusing on the philosophical thought of **Luce Irigaray**. With its post-structuralist foundations, Irigaray's writings are a place for thinking through the meaning and application of difference and disruption such that it challenges the dominance of masculine patriarchal order. What we arrive at is a culture of difference. We learn that difference and disruption is not based on outright dualistic opposition but on a more nuanced acknowledgement of the existence of different sexes, bodies, forms of desire and ways of knowing. Such acknowledgment requires that the suppression of femininity and difference be over-turned as part of a wider rejection of the limiting (suppressing) effects of masculine thought. This is exemplified by Irigaray's critique of psychoanalysis as a system that constructs and reproduces patriarchal forms of subjectivity that reinforce the phallocentric nature that governs dominant discourses (a critique for which, as Sheena Vachhani notes, Irigaray was effectively exiled from the psychoanalytic establishment). It is also seen in the practice of reclaiming and then redrawing essentialist characteristics of the feminine to subvert them. Sheena Vachhani presents the writings of Luce Irigaray as fluid and mellifluous engagements with possibility that challenge the dominance of masculine rationality in organization studies in favour of more embodied accounting for, and use of, the feminine voice.

In Chapter 6 by Ajnesh Prasad, Paulina Segarra and Cristian E. Villanueva, we are reminded of the ways in which ethnocentrism can effectively subjugate and objectify the 'other' as part of culturally embedded biases and practices. Succinctly outlining a critique of second-wave white Western feminism, they draw our attention to the ways in which **Donna Haraway** developed theoretical insights that disavowed the ethnocentrism underlying universal truth-claims, while at the same time enabling feminists to engage responsibly in discourses about 'other' women in an effort to catalyse social change. In a move that is echoed in many of the writings in this series, Donna Haraway makes the case for an embodied understanding of the world around us that is objective in so far as it is grounded in our sensory systems, while being contextually sensitive such that transcendental or universal claims are not made. The resulting 'feminist objectivity' sees knowledge as situated, partial and locatable. Enacted through passionate detachment, such knowledge is held answerable for its claims while also offering the possibility of holding cultural practices to account. Prasad, Segarra and Villanueva then consider how such theorising has informed the use of post-colonial theory in organization and management studies such that it is possible to engage with the 'other' while attending to the concerns of positionality and representation. The result is a more nuanced and reflexive engagement with and through the cultures of self and other.

Taken together the above works reimagine what it means to organize and manage in contemporary workplaces and organizations. In so doing, the authors invite readers in their multiplicity to rethink their own experiences of management and culture to embrace perspectives that reject totalising accounts of culture in favour of perspectives that are multiple, partial, critical and constructive. Culture as understood through women writers is embodied – it is not constructed without people, and the diversity of experience and bodies lies at the heart of understanding culture. This is a book for those who want to identify organizational norms, appreciate practices of organizing and managing in their various and shifting shades, and be able to critique them. Understanding culture as an exercise of power enables readers to appreciate the ways in which organizations shape people in their workplaces, as well as the ways in which people resist organizational norms. This fourth book in the series provides the most interesting and timely theorising on culture management and organizing.

2 Joanne Martin

Lotte Holck and Sara L. Muhr

Joanne Martin is the Fred H. Merrill Professor of Organizational Behavior, Emerita at the Graduate School of Business, Stanford University. Martin holds a BA in fine art from Smith College, where she studied woodcutting with Leonard Baskin, and a PhD in social psychology from Harvard University. As a social psychologist, who critically investigates key issues of organization studies, Martin has received numerous awards, including the Centennial Medal from the Graduate School of Arts and Sciences, Harvard University, for research-based contributions to society[1]. She was the first woman at Stanford Graduate School of Business to earn tenure and was for a long time the only woman in any business school department there. For this reason, the Centennial Medal was particularly important to her, and the speech at the award ceremony was focused primarily on her work on gender and served as a door-opener for other female scholars and legitimised feminist scholarship.

While, as we will show in this chapter, she has worked extensively on issues of social justice, feminist theory and (gendered) aspects of academic careers and research processes, she is mostly known for her comprehensive work on organizational culture. In a blurb on the back cover of Martin's key book from 1992, *Cultures in Organizations: Three Perspectives*, Rosabeth Moss Kanter writes: "Joanne Martin is an astute and insightful analyst of organizational culture, who continually probes below the surface to reveal the reality buried beneath official pronouncements". The chapter aims to draw attention to the important work of Joanne Martin by mapping and discussing her three perspectives on culture – those of integration, differentiation and fragmentation – and illustrating their relevance for organization studies. In addition, we will also draw attention to other important aspects of her work on social (in)justice, gender (in)equality and (gendered) aspects of academic careers and research processes. To keep in mind the feminist goal of this volume, however, we have decided to focus mostly on Martin's work on gender (in)equality and (gendered) aspects of academic careers and research processes and how both intersect with her theory of culture. By doing this, we highlight Martin's consistent simultaneous commitment to holism on the one hand, and the disruption of unitary fantasies on the other. We will end by discussing how Martin's cultural theory together with her feminist work can be a powerful combination for scholars who want to engage with an elaborate and helpful organization theory of culture, supplemented by a (possibly radical) feminist change agenda.

The chapter draws on a close reading of her written work as well as an email conversation with Martin about her scholarly work. We are forever grateful for Martin's very helpful comments and feedback throughout the entire process.

(Meta)theory of culture

Joanne Martin's theory of culture in organizations was first introduced in her book *Cultures in Organizations: Three Perspectives* from 1992 and later more fully explicated in *Organizational Culture: Mapping the Terrain* from 2002. The 1992 book was part of what has later been called 'the cultural turn', and the 2002 book is a revision and expansion of the theory presented in the 1992 book, partly based on the many scholars who picked up on and operationalised Martin's culture theory as presented in her 1992 book (e.g. Gherardi, 1995; Kreiner and Schultz, 1995; Schultz and Hatch, 1996). This gives Martin's theory a large empirical base, which she eloquently recognises and incorporates in her 2002 book. Martin's theory of culture – as presented in both books as well as in many articles – offers a unique, multidimensional and comprehensive perspective on organizational culture that captures the complexity inherent in a culture analysis. The book presents three prevailing perspectives in organizational culture research: integration, differentiation and fragmentation. Martin argues that a comprehensive approach towards a holistic understanding of an organization's cultural context needs to consider all three perspectives (Martin, 2002). Importantly, all three perspectives are equal, and none can be preferred or neglected. For analytical purposes, however, we will go through the three perspectives one by one.

Integration

Culture from an integration perspective is what people in a group or organization share; it is the social glue that ties the organization together. An integration view assumes consensus among all members of the organization, who supposedly share basic convictions and interpret cultural manifestations in a similar way. Integration thus necessitates the absence of ambiguity and uncertainty. Most researchers who adopt the integration perspective argue that a unitary organizational culture encourages cohesion and commitment. A homogeneous, unitary culture supposedly functions as an organizational stabiliser that produces desirable work behaviours among organizational members, since they work together in harmony and consensus (Martin, 2002). The integration view also adopts a static image of identity. Like the organization, individual identity is regarded as a fixed, unambiguous entity occurring within clearly defined boundaries (Martin, 2002).

The integration perspective is dominated by a clear leader-centred focus, whereby culture is initiated and defined by top management and integrated throughout the organization to promote organizational efficiency and pro-ductivity. The most popular manifestation of the integration perspective is Schein's three levels of culture, in which a strong, unified culture gives rise to a coherent and strategic relationship between artefacts, values and basic assumptions (Schein, 2010[1885]). Schein's integrative approach rests on the assumption that homogeneity is possible and productive (Schein, 2010[1885]). Martin does not disagree with Schein's three levels of cul-ture and the importance of the links between artefacts, values and basic assumptions. However, she disagrees about the possibility of *only* having an integrated, homogeneous culture. This is usually seen from a managerial perspective, disregarding the fact that organizations will always also be dif-ferentiated and fragmented.

While the integration approach provides easy answers for practitioners, due to complexity reduction Martin insists on its limitations. First, integra-tion ignores and excludes inconsistencies and ambiguities occurring within cultural boundaries (Martin, 2002). Second, a clear and static definition of culture and identity neglects the constant change inherent in organiza-tions *and* individuals. An overemphasis on organization-wide consensus marginalises group members whose values and demographic identities are different from an assumed norm, by denying and therefore silencing any perspectives that do not conform with those of the majority (Martin, 2002). Given the dominance of white men in organizational hierarchies, an integra-tion perspective often results in emphasising male viewpoints and silencing those of women and minorities. Following this argument, an integration perspective runs the risk of perpetuating dominant (managerial) views and existing power structures within an organization.

Differentiation

Most researchers who adopt the integration perspective perceive strong unitary cultures as providing cultural clarity and consistency among mem-bers with the ambition to enhance organizational performance. In contrast, researchers who adopt the differentiation perspective focus on the existence of inconsistency and disagreement in the form of subcultures in order to highlight the political nature of organizational culture (Martin, 2002). While the differentiation perspective does not deny the potential existence of organization-wide values and interests, it focuses on subgroups with a homogeneous point of view that may differ from a standardised norm imposed by those in power.

Theories stressing differentiation move away from a transmission of a solid state of 'culture' towards uncovering and analysing the political processes and dynamics that come to constitute, reproduce and disrupt cultural relations and thus form subcultures (e.g. Meyerson and Martin, 1987). These subcultures coexist sometimes in harmony, sometimes in conflict, and sometimes in indifference or independence. Subcultures consist of a subset of an organization's members who identify as a distinct group within the organization and routinely act on the basis of their unique collective understandings (Hatch and Cunliffe, 2006). Hence subcultures may form around similar interests within an organization and may reflect shared professional, gendered, racial, ethnic or occupational identities. Alternatively, they may form based on the familiarity that develops when employees interact frequently, for example, when they share space or equipment.

Martin argues that subcultures can react to each other in one of four ways: *dominant, enhancing, orthogonal* or *countercultural* (Louis, 1983). Typically, the *dominant* subculture in an organization is put forward by top management, and therefore it is often referred to as the corporate culture, even though it may be more correct to call it a corporate subculture. Furthermore,

> an *enhancing* subculture would exist in an organizational enclave in which adherence to the core values of the dominant culture would be more fervent than in the rest of the organization. In an *orthogonal* subculture, the members would simultaneously accept the core values of the dominant culture and a separate, unconflicting set of values particular to themselves.
>
> (Martin and Siehl, 1990: 54, authors' emphasis)

Finally, *countercultures* hold values and beliefs that actively challenge corporate cultures (Hatch and Cunliffe, 2006; Louis, 1983).

Culture analysis conducted using the differentiation perspective focuses on the inconsistency between managerial/organizational rhetoric and cultural forms. As Martin explains: "Analysis of inconsistencies in the interpretation of cultural forms, such as stories, rituals, and jargon, often reveals an 'underbelly' of conflict that is not acknowledged in managerial rhetoric that stresses teamwork, harmony, egalitarianism, or cooperation" (Martin, 1992: 87). In fact, according to many differentiation researchers, the integration perspective is a myth, which is created for the benefit of top management to hide the contradictions and conflicts that inevitably exist in any organizational culture (Martin, 2002). The differentiation perspective does not deny the existence of similarities and consistency; it explores the arguments and discourses of the subcultural members, who interpret things differently. Consequently, many analyses applying a differentiation perspective distinguish employee interests from those of management, which include efforts of control by and resistance to a dominant corporate culture (e.g. Contu, 2008; Nentwich and Hoyer, 2013).

Critics of the differentiation view argue together with Martin that – as within the integration perspective – the all-too-clear definition of culture presents an oversimplification, as it neglects the complexity and constant change inherent in organizations as well as individuals. Neither the integration nor the differentiation perspective take into consideration that boundaries between cultures and subcultures are far from stable, but instead are characterised by permeability and flux: neither of the two perspectives offers acknowledgement of the inescapable ambiguities of organizations (Martin, 2002).

Fragmentation

While the integration view assumes that an organizational culture can be defined as singular and stable, thwarting ambiguity, the differentiation view assumes that ambiguity can be channelled outside subcultures. In contrast, the fragmentation perspective focuses on how organizational culture is internally contradictory, ambiguous, multiple and in a constant flux – but without losing cultural meaning (Meyerson and Martin, 1987). In the fragmentation perspective, ambiguity is regarded "as the essence of culture" (Martin, 1992: 118). Martin defines ambiguity as consisting of three elements: uncertainty, contradiction and confusion. Uncertainty is externally caused (e.g. environmental/market influences), contradiction is internal, within one's mind (e.g. double meanings of things) and confusion is caused by ignorance or lack of information.

Following the fragmentation perspective, alliances or coalitions (central in the differentiation perspective) never stabilise into subcultures and certainly not into an integrated culture. In research done from a fragmentation perspective, there is no unity of understanding, no consensus or affinity, even within subcultures, since understandings are temporary, and interpretations alter incessantly. The focus is therefore on exploring the complexity of relationships between different cultural expressions (Martin, 1992: 131) and how individual identities modify and develop through such relationships. From a fragmentation perspective, individuals constantly fluctuate

> among diverse and changing identities, pulled by issues and events to focus on one aspect of the self rather than another – temporarily. ... Subcultures, then, are reconceptualized as fleeting, issue-specific coalitions that may or may not have a similar configuration in the future. This is not simply a failure to achieve (sub)cultural consensus in a particular context; from the fragmentation perspective this is the most consensus possible in any context.
>
> (Martin, 1992: 156)

Organizations, environments and groups are thus seen as constantly changing, as individuals hold fragmented and fluctuating self-concepts together with "issue-specific coalitions" (Martin, 1992: 157). Consequently, Martin suggests the following definition of culture based on a fragmentation perspective:

> An organization [culture] is a web of individuals, sporadically and loosely connected by their changing positions on a variety of issues. Their involvement, their subcultural identities, and their individual self-definitions fluctuate, depending on which issues are activated at a given moment.
>
> (Martin, 1992: 153)

From a fragmentation perspective, organizations are perceived as multicultural and fluctuating, riddled by constant ambiguity and multiple, shifting and opposing opinions and perceptions. This is caused by societal problems that we cannot fully understand and cannot universally solve, e.g. poverty, racism, crime, etc., which permeate the workplace and are reproduced by workplace relations and encounters. Martin explains how race, ethnicity, gender, occupation, hierarchical position and other identifying characteristics coexist within each member of an organization. Accordingly, overlapping allegiances with others might infinitely change organizational subcultures in response to ever-changing issues that appear in organizational discourses. Topical organizational issues at one point of time will draw out one configuration of a member's identity, while in the next a different configuration may be called upon.

With the fragmentation perspective, Martin subscribes to arguments of critical cultural scholars highlighting how organizational culture might work as a powerful tool that helps the 'dominant coalition' to mask their manipulation and control over the rest of the organization (see also the work of e.g. Kunda and Van Maanen, 1999). As Martin and Siehl (1990: 52) state: "Cultures serve as organizational control mechanisms, informally approving or prohibiting ... patterns of behaviour." However, from a fragmentation perspective, power is not seen as *localised* at the top management level or at the subcultural level (following Schein). Instead, power is identified as in constant and changeable flux rather than as a stable unity identifiable at certain key points in the organization.

Adopting the fragmentation perspective, Martin (1987) offers a critique of how culture research in general has neglected ambiguity: "Ambiguity is banished from the kingdom of culture. Culture becomes that which is clear" (4). Instead she argues:

> Ambiguity is an inescapable element of any organizational culture – whether that ambiguity is received with distaste, tolerated with reluctance, or welcomed as a source of creativity and freedom ... any description of these cultures that excludes ambiguities would be incomplete, misleading, and of very limited utility.
>
> (Martin, 1992: 5)

Martin suggests that

> the definitions of culture offered [by existing literature] are inappropriate for describing most contemporary organizational cultures. Such definitions may be throw-backs to a long-lost or possibly illusory way of life (the isolated Pacific archipelago, untouched by western influence), where lucid understandings, clear solutions and shared understandings were abundant.
>
> (Martin, 1987: 15)

As she later succinctly explains: "until organisational researchers incorporate ambiguity into our approaches to studying culture, we run the risk of misrepresenting our informants, misleading those who read our work, and deceiving ourselves" (Martin, 1992: 16). Even though Martin first offered this critique more than 30 years ago and it subsequently has been theoretically and empirically expanded and extended by decades of research by Martin (as explained above) and many others (e.g. Gherardi, 1995; Kreiner and Schultz, 1995; Schultz and Hatch, 1996), this approach to studying culture still holds value considering the contemporary prevalence of the integration perspective on culture.

Beyond the three perspectives

The most revolutionary and significant contribution of Martin's culture theory is her argument that all three perspectives must be applied *simultaneously* to fully capture the many layers of fluid corporate cultures that any organization necessarily consists of; to fully appreciate organizational culture is to identify and reveal its inherent multidimensionality and overlapping contradictory complexities. With *Culture in Organizations: Three Perspectives*, Martin endeavours to develop a meta-theory on organizational culture. This is also how her culture theory, which she classifies into her three perspectives, significantly differs from other culture theories. Martin underlines how cultural research can be seen as a conversation: "All too often, disagreements among cultural researchers take the form of a debate about which theory or method is the one best way" (Martin, 1995: 230). *Culture in Organizations: Three Perspectives* is, in Martin's (1995: 230) own words, "an attempt to find alternative ways of writing about culture that are more tolerant—even expressive of—opposing views". Martin goes on: "The three perspectives, however, and their critical and managerial variants, could be reconceptualised – not as competing alternatives – but as complementary parts of a meta-theory" (Martin et al., 2006: 18). Martin has highlighted that "cultural theory would be enriched if our texts were truly polyphonic, with informants and researchers struggling collaboratively to develop shared understandings and texts that preserve difference of opinion and ambiguity" (Martin, 1995: 231); hence, the very essence and strength of Martin's culture theory is to insist on going beyond the three separate perspectives. A multi-perspective view on culture that forms a holistic understanding of an organization's cultural context, and considers all three perspectives, is advocated (Martin, 2002): Combining the three perspectives will reveal the blind spots of each single perspective and perhaps open the door to other perspectives not yet articulated.

'Other' writings

Although Martin is mostly known for her work on culture, she has an impressive record in feminist critiques of gender (in)equality as well as social (in)justice. This work deserves to be highlighted not only because it is a powerful body of work, but also because the thinking that underlies this body of work is fundamental for the way her meta-theory on culture has developed and must be comprehended: Knowing and appreciating these other aspects of her academic work makes it easier to understand and utilise the specificities of her culture framework.

We will go through her work on gender (in)equality and the (gendered) research process below. However, to contextualise this work we will initially draw attention to a book chapter on feminist theory and critical theory, which is part of Alvesson and Willmott's (2003) edited volume *Studying Management Critically*. We believe this piercing critique that Martin (2003) directs towards scholars of critical theory is fundamental to her entire thinking and offers a key to how her work on culture, gender inequality and the (gendered) research process intersect. In her critique, Martin (2003) succinctly shows how critical theorists' claim to criticality is problematic due to their avoidance of issues like gender, race and sexuality. She demonstrates how concerns of critical theory overlap with those of feminist theory; the two bodies of work 'just' tend to place their focus on different items. While

> feminist theorists use sex and gender as the fulcrum of their analysis (usually, but not always, with secondary emphasis on class, race, and ethnicity), ... critical theorists often place class at the crux of their analysis, with sex, gender, race and ethnicity being less emphasized.
>
> (Martin, 2003: 66–67)

In her analysis of why the two traditions, despite several similarities, have developed into two separate disciplines, she poses the intriguing question of why edited volumes on critical theory almost solely consist of male authors, citing men, while rarely including issues of gender and sexuality, or inspiration from feminist theory. Concurrently Martin states:

> When critical theory publications do offer an extended discussion of feminist ideas, it is often relegated to a footnote, a parenthetical aside, a list of 'also relevant' types of literature, or at best a separate chapter – forms of marginalization that can inadvertently serve as a justification for excluding gender issues from the rest of the text.
>
> (Martin, 2003: 79)

This point is particularly sharp, as this was exactly the status that Martin's chapter was given in the book these very words were written in. Alvesson and Willmott's edited book only included two female co-authors and then Martin's (single-authored) chapter on feminist theory. Her point is even more valid if we take into consideration the predecessor to the 2003 book that Martin's chapter appears in. The predecessor, *Critical Management Studies*, edited by the same authors in 1992, had zero female authors and no chapters on feminist theory or gender, race or sexuality.

In the chapter, Martin (2003) explores why critical and feminist theories have been and continue to be separated. She lists four 'reasons' why critical theory has not embraced feminist theory and then argues against these reasons: 1) Feminist theory focuses primarily on privileged women and therefore fails to critique hegemony (Martin, 2003: 79); 2) feminist theory seeks to reverse gender inequalities by privileging women over men (Martin, 2003: 83); 3) feminist theory is incomplete, or narrow, unless it includes the study of men, the constraints of masculinity and relations between genders

(Martin, 2003: 84); and 4) critical theory is broader because it considers abstract topics, such as technocracy and ecological problems, that pertain to both genders (Martin, 2003: 84). She is particularly focused on the last point (that critical theory is broader than feminist theory) probably because this point is directly belittling feminist theory. She cites Alvesson and Willmott:

> [Critical theory] has the strength of being sufficiently broad to serve as a source of critical reflection on a large number of central issues in management studies: epistemological issues, notions of rationality and progress, technocracy and social engineering, autonomy and control, communicative action, power and ideology. In comparison Marxist, Foucauldian and feminist perspectives are more specialized and restricted.
>
> (Alvesson and Willmott, 1992: 9, cited in Martin, 2003: 85)

To refute this prevailing position, she demonstrates how feminist theory is relevant for every topic in the edited volume: gender, race and sexuality are not an 'and', but human conditions, and thus by definition are present and relevant no matter whether one theorises on and discusses accounting, ethics or management practice. Accordingly, Martin emphasises how critical theory could be strengthened by systematically addressing issues of gender, race and sexuality, and she has spent a considerable amount of her scholarly work on deconstructing the assumed gender-neutral and race-neutral arguments (see Martin and Harder, 1994; Pettigrew and Martin, 1987a, 1987b) pertaining to critical theory while insisting on the benefit of merging critical and feminist scholarship. As explained in the introduction, we will keep the focus on how Martin's feminist work intersects with her work on culture and the (gendered) research process, and will not go into detail on her work on social (in)justice but limit ourselves to her work on gender inequality, which we turn to next. Nevertheless, it is paramount to stress that her early work on social (in)justice included critical analysis of race and ethnicity, which without doubt must have influenced the way her later feminist work materialised.

Gender inequality

A considerable amount of Martin's work has been committed to breaking the academic silence in relation to gender inequality. Accordingly, Martin has, together with Debra Meyerson, analysed how micropolitical processes undermine formal power which leaves women disempowered – despite having considerable formal power (Martin and Meyerson, 1998). In the same article, they also stressed how employees form alliances and act

strategically to pursue individual opportunities that reproduce gender inequality through a series of institutionalised practices (Martin and Meyerson,
1998). Martin has, in similar ways all through her career, admirably fought
a battle to reveal how theories and data are not gender neutral, as well as
how gender research is marginalised in academia. Her hope is

> that familiarity with a range of these kinds of analyses will tempt
> organizational researchers who have never before considered gender-
> related issues to question whether gender might be at work in what they
> read, what they teach, and how they do research and develop theory.
>
> (Martin, 2000: 208)

Martin has been an early leading voice in exposing the inequality in academic institutions. "Institutionalized practices and structures contribute
to sex inequality in universities, gendered definitions of faculty jobs and
gendered limitations to knowledge in the field of organizational studies",
she observes (Martin, 1994: 401), while pointing out how few academic
handbooks, textbooks and other key texts include women researchers. In a
sense, this present book series is trying to make up for that, although – as
Martin also points out – it would have been more powerful had it been main-
streamed into any text, not 'just' a book series on women writers. However,
it is the hope of these writers that this book series will at least make women
writers, such as Joanne Martin herself, more visible and hence included
in future mainstream collections. As Martin (1994) underlines, changing
the number of women isn't enough, as sex inequality persists despite the
influx of women into lower academic positions (e.g. female PhD students).
For example, while the influx of academic women at the entry level of the
academic hierarchy has increased considerably, the upper level of academia
(senior faculty as well as management) remains overwhelmingly (white
and) male.

Her focus on gender and academia has encouraged Martin to reinterpret
and deconstruct classic texts. One example is Martin and Knopoff's (1997)
critical feminist reading of the gender implications of Weber's apparently
gender-neutral language. They demonstrate how despite Weber's awareness of class differences, gender is not mentioned. Of course, as the authors
also note, Weber wrote at a time when women weren't allowed to work.
However, their critique touches upon how Weber's work has been translated
into presumed gender neutrality within current scholarship on, for example,
bureaucracy. They discuss the implications of this omission, and deconstruct key terms in Weber's texts – such as hierarchy, division of labour
and impersonality – in order to expose the gender inequality that is reproduced in a presumably gender-neutral text: "deconstruction is suspicious

of dichotomies, in part because such distinctions exaggerate differences, deny similarities and ambiguities and omit all that does not fit" (Martin and Knopoff, 1997: 34). In this way, Martin's way of using deconstruction fits very well with her insistence on the simultaneity of integration, differentiation and fragmentation. As an alternative to a Weberian bureaucracy, Martin and Knopoff (1997) suggest the feminist organization while considering its pros and cons. Martin et al. (1998) go on to explore Weber's notion of impersonality in their work on bounded emotionality in The Body Shop International. They demonstrate how

> impersonal criteria for making decisions and restraints on emotional expression at work have long been the hallmarks of bureaucracy (e.g., Weber, 1946, 1981). Recent work has broken this emotional taboo, exploring how certain organizations require the expression of particular emotions at work to maximize organizational productivity.
>
> (Martin et al., 1998: 429)

Accordingly, they point out how bounded emotionality can be a dangerous form of organizational control, and hence they contribute to research on culture and normative control, supplementing the work of Kunda and Van Maanen (1989).

One of Martin's (1990) strengths is her use of illustrative stories, as it provides the reader of her texts with persuasive illustrations of her theoretical arguments. One utterly memorable story is her deconstruction of a male CEO's tale of how he and his firm helped a female employee balance private life and work around the birth of her baby. She does so by retelling first the exact same story, but replacing the female protagonist, a pregnant woman getting a caesarean timed to fit the launch of a new product, with a man rescheduling his coronary bypass operation to fit the product launch. By retelling the story in this way, Martin (1990) exposes the absurdity in the way the original story is told – but also how assumed gender neutrality is not gender neutral at all.

Martin (2000) continues the deconstructive work published in her earlier career and develops the idea of *re-visioning* to further expose and undo gender inequality. Besides her above-mentioned work on Weber and her analysis of emotional expression in organizations, she also highlights Acker and Van Houten's (1992) gendered analysis of the Hawthorne experiments and Crozier's field studies. This is to display the impact of segregated gender composition of test groups (with women workers and male supervisors) and of highly sex-segregated workplaces acting as case 'organizations' – factors that are not considered in the original texts. As Martin (2000: 210) muses, "to write of these structures and processes in gender-neutral terms, as if the wide-spread occupational sex segregation did not affect and exacerbate these dynamics, seems questionable". Martin (2000) goes on to explore how theoretical analyses of concepts like dependency, stress and burnout, rationality and emotionality have been analysed differently alongside stereotypes of masculinity and femininity, depending on whether the research subject was a man or a woman. This is an impressively varied body of work, and her overall ambition thus seems to be to make researchers aware of how disregarding the gendered dimensions of analysis risks falling back on stereotypes that impact interpretations of assumed gender-neutral data in gendered ways, thereby angling the results and colouring the conclusions. She ends up proposing a future research agenda with the ambition to reinterpret the 'classic' texts through the lenses of gender and race.

Based on her decades of gender research, Martin pleads for a feminist change agenda in one of her latest texts: "Gender researchers need to go beyond body counts and studies that document discrimination and inequality, we need to refocus our research agenda on change ... building theories that will help change the inequalities that have been so fully documented" (Martin and Meyerson, 2008: 553). She thus calls for a change agenda that both feminist and critical scholars agree on but still struggle to unfold.

On (gendered) aspects of academic careers and research processes

Martin has devoted a great deal of her scholarly career to writings that criticise the academic process – both the institutional process of recruitment and advancement, the process of career development, and the academic production process (or research and publication) itself. Although this is still debated to this day – especially within critical management studies and poststructuralist critiques of the objective truth claims of the scientific model of empirical research (see for example Butler et al., 2017) – Martin had, in 1981, already questioned the so-called 'rational' model for research processes. She argued that the 'rational model' is assumed to 1) formulate a theoretical problem; 2) select an appropriate research method(s), design and conduct a study; 3) analyse and interpret results; and 4) use results to confirm/deny theory (Martin, 1981: 131). Based on March and colleagues' notion of garbage-can decision making, she suggests that the research process and the development of a research problem do not have to be 'rational'. Instead, they can follow a garbage-can model, whereby problems are produced in advance and matched with research agendas, just as problems can be produced in organizations and matched with decision making. She thus argues for non-theoretical causes for problem identification. As such, she had already committed 40 years ago to a radical showdown with traditional research processes. Martin is however rarely mentioned in the recent debate on criticality and research relevance.

Co-authored with Shelly Taylor, Martin has written a wonderful text on how to practically navigate 'life in academia' (Taylor and Martin, 1986), which has become a much-cited underground classic. The text, in fact, became so popular that in 2002 Taylor and Martin published a more accessible – and slightly edited – version as a Stanford research paper[2]. As they, with a lovely touch of humour, write in the 2002 version: "When you pride yourself on your research record, it is unnerving to discover that one of the most frequently cited papers you have ever written is a 'how to' piece" (Taylor and Martin, 2002: 1). But it is with good reason that it became so popular, as the text is a warm but honest explanation of the ups and downs of academic life. In fact, after reading it, one of the authors of this chapter immediately sent the text to all PhD students and junior faculty in her department. In the text, Taylor and Martin compare an academic career to a marathon that comprises three stages: getting started, hitting your stride and hitting the wall (and the rest of your career). They outline the academic tasks ahead of young (and more senior) scholars, and comment on issues like what's a 'fair share', what to avoid and how (if?) it is all 'worth it'. The text is written with warmth, sincerity and humour, not least the very last sentence, in which they argue in favour of going somewhere nice for conferences:

> Eventually you will get invited to better places and when you are, this will give you an opportunity to explore an exciting new city. Make sure you take the time to do so. This hedonistic approach to work is important to us. It explains why we work so hard to manage our time and it explains why, from time to time, we abandon our rational plans to do exactly what we feel we would enjoy – like writing this chapter.

The fact that Martin, together with Taylor, takes the time to write a text like this is, for us, representative of most of Martin's work, which is socially engaged, caring and committed to change.

Conclusion – the future of Martin and organization studies

It is important to include Martin in this book for many reasons. However, two particular reasons stand out. Firstly, her work on organizational culture is highly relevant and usable in today's organizations, which are riddled with complexity, ambiguity and fluidity that both researchers and practitioners necessarily must consider. Personally, we use Martin's work when we teach both undergraduate, graduate and MBA students and we have yet to meet a student who doesn't find the three perspectives framework useful – whether for a theoretical or empirical analysis. Thus, with this chapter we hope that more teachers, researchers and practitioners will draw on her theory of culture rather than other, simpler frameworks that are often included in business school curricula. Secondly, even if people are aware of her work on culture, Martin's work on gender, feminist theory and academia is often overlooked. With this chapter, our second ambition is to shed light on the importance of this part of her work. Again, we doubt you'll meet a student, who does not find her deconstruction of organizational taboos eye-opening (Martin, 1990). Overall, she persuasively and in a timely fashion reminds us of the importance of the intersections of gendered, raced and classed ideologies and provides us with frameworks for their deconstruction and undoing, which are equally valid today as when she wrote them several decades ago.

To paraphrase Martin (2000: 209), we should all fight the disgraceful and disappointing fact that gender and diversity research remains a separate and inferior kind of knowledge. In addition, it is pivotal to avoid preaching to the converted. Reaching out to and getting included in mainstream research is crucial according to Martin. Martin's work on culture, which is generally accepted (although not as popular as, for example, Schein's) and forms part of mainstream organization studies while drawing on her work on combating (gender) inequality and (social) injustice, shows a powerful example of how to do this.

Acknowledgement

This chapter is part of the research project 'Leading Cultural Diversity Ethically' financed by the Ragnar Söderberg foundation: www.ragnarsoderbergsstiftelse.se

Notes

1 www.gsb.stanford.edu/faculty-research/faculty/joanne-martin
2 The research paper can be downloaded here: www.gsb.stanford.edu/faculty-r esearch/faculty/joanne-martin

Recommended reading

Original text by Joanne Martin

Meyerson, D. and Martin, J. (1987). Cultural change: An integration of three different views. *Journal of Management Studies*, 24(6): 623–647.

Martin, J. (2003). Feminist theory and critical theory: Unexplored synergies. In: M. Alvesson and H. Willmott (eds.), *Studying Management Critically*, pp. 66–91. London: SAGE.

Key academic text

Taylor, B.C., Irvin, L.R. and Wieland, S.M. (2006). Checking the map: Critiquing Joanne Martin's metatheory of organizational culture and its uses in communication research. *Communication Theory*, 16(3): 304–332.

Accessible resource

Hatch, M.J. and Cunliffe, A.L. (2006). Chapter 6 on 'organizational cultue'. In: M.J. Hatch and A.L. Cunliffe (eds.), *Organization Theory: Modern, Symbolic, and Postmodern Perspectives*. Oxford: Oxford University Press.

References

Alvesson, M. and Willmott, H. (Eds.). (1992). *Critical Management Studies*. Newbury Park, CA: SAGE Publications.

Alvesson, M. and Willmott, H. (2003). *Studying Management Critically*. London: SAGE Publications.

Butler, N., Delaney, H. and Śliwa, M. (2017). The labour of academia. *Ephemera*, 17(3): 467–480.

Contu, A. (2008). Decaf resistance: On misbehavior, cynicism, and desire in liberal workplaces. *Management Communication Quarterly*, 21(3): 364–379.

Gherardi, S. (1995). When will he say "today the plates are soft?": The management of ambiguity and situated decision-making. *Studies in Cultures, Organizations and Societies*, 1(1): 9–27.

Hatch, M.J. and Cunliffe, A.L. (2006). *Organization Theory: Modern, Symbolic, and Postmodern Perspectives*. Oxford: Oxford University Press.

Kreiner, K. and Schultz, M. (1995). Soft cultures: The symbolism of cross-border organizing. *Studies in Cultures, Organizations and Societies*, 1(1): 63–81.

Kunda, G. and van Maanen, J. (1999). Changing scripts at work: Managers and professionals. *The Annals of the American Academy of Political and Social Science*, 561(1): 64–80.

Louis, M. (1983). Sourcing workplace cultures: Why, when, and how? In: R. Kilmann (ed.), *Managing Corporate Cultures*, pp. 126–136. San Francisco: Jossey-Bass.

Martin, J. (1981). A garbage can model of the psychological research process. *American Behavioral Scientist*, 25(2): 131–151.

Martin, J. (1987). A black hole: Ambiguity in organizational culture. Stanford University. Working paper 946.

Martin, J. (1990). Deconstructing organizational taboos: The suppression of gender conflict in organizations. *Organization Science*, 1(4): 339–359.

Martin, J. (1992). *Cultures in Organizations: Three Perspectives*. Oxford: Oxford University Press.

Martin, J. (1994). The organization of exclusion: The institutionalization of sex inequality, gendered faculty jobs, and gendered knowledge in organizational theory and research. *Organization*, 1(2): 401–431.

Martin, J. (1995). The style and structure of cultures in organizations: Three perspectives. *Organization Science*, 6(2): 230–232.

Martin, J. (2000). Hidden gendered assumptions in mainstream organizational theory and research. *Journal of Management Inquiry*, 9(2): 207–216.

Martin, J. (2002). *Organizational Culture: Mapping the Terrain*. London: Sage publications.

Martin, J. (2003). Feminist theory and critical theory: Unexplored synergies. In: M. Alvesson and H. Willmott (eds.), *Studying Management Critically*, pp. 66–91. London: SAGE.

Martin, J., Frost, P.J. and O'Neill, O.A. (2006). Organizational culture: Beyond struggles for intellectual dominance. In: Stewart R. Clegg, Cynthia Hardy, Thomas B. Lawrence, and Walter R. Nord (eds.), *The SAGE Handbook of Organization Studies*. Newbury Park, CA: SAGE.

Martin, J. and Harder, J.W. (1994). Bread and roses: Justice and the distribution of financial and socioemotional rewards in organizations. *Social Justice Research*, 7(3): 241–264.

Martin, J. and Knopoff, K. (1997). The gendered implications of apparently gender-neutral organizational theory: Re-reading Weber. In: Andrea Larson and R. Edward Freeman (eds.), *Ruffin Lecture Series, III: Business Ethics and Women's Studies*, pp. 30–49. Oxford, England: Oxford University Press.

Martin, J., Knopoff, K. and Beckman, C. (1998). An alternative to bureaucratic impersonality and emotional labor: Bounded emotionality at The Body Shop. *Administrative Science Quarterly*, 43(2): 429–469.

Martin, J. and Meyerson, D. (1998). Women and power: Conformity, resistance, and disorganized co-action. In: Roderick M. Kramer and Dr. Margaret A. Neale (eds.), *Power and Influence in Organizations*, pp. 311–348. London: SAGE Publications.

Martin, J. and Meyerson, D. (2008). Gender inequity and the need to study change. In: Daved Barry and Hans Hansen (eds.), *The Sage Handbook of New Approaches in Management and Organisation*, pp. 552–554. London: SAGE Publications.

Martin, J. and Siehl, C. (1990). Organizational culture: A key to financial performance? In: Benjamin Schneider (author), *Organizational Climate and Culture*, pp. 241–281. San Franscisco: Jossey-Bass.

Meyerson, D. and Martin, J. (1987). Cultural change: An integration of three different views. *Journal of Management Studies*, 24(6): 623–647.

Nentwich, J. and Hoyer, P. (2013). Part-time work as practising resistance: The power of counter-arguments. *British Journal of Management*, 24(4): 557–570.

Pettigrew, T.F. and Martin, J. (1987a). Shaping the organizational context for black American inclusion. *Journal of Social Issues*, 43(1): 41–78.

Pettigrew, T.F. and Martin, J. (1987b). The fruits of critical discussion: A reply to the commentators. *Journal of Social Issues*, 43(1): 145–156.

Schein, E.H. (2010 [1985]). *Organizational Culture and Leadership*, 4th edition. San Francisco: John Wiley & Sons.

Schultz, M. and Hatch, M. (1996). Living with multiple paradigms: The case of paradigm interplay in organizational culture studies. *Academy of Management Review*, 21(2): 529–557.

Taylor, S.E. and Martin, J. (1986). The present-minded professor: Controlling one's career. In: J.M. Darley, M.P. Zanna and H.L. Roediger, *The Complete Academic: A Career Guide*, pp. 23–60. New York: Random House.

Taylor, S.E. and Martin, J. (1986). The present-minded professor: Controlling one's career. In: M.P. Zanna and J.M. Darley (eds.), *The Complete Academic: A Practical Guide for the Beginning Social Scientist*. New York: Random House.

Taylor, S.E. and Martin, J. (2002). The academic marathon: Managing the academic career. Stanford Working Paper [www.gsb.stanford.edu/faculty-research/faculty/joanne-martin].

3   Mary Douglas

The cultural and material manifestations of dirt and dirty work

Ruth Simpson and Jason Hughes

In this chapter we explore the work of Mary Douglas, arguably the most widely read social anthropologist of her generation, through her seminal text *Purity and Danger* (Douglas, 1966). We examine the influence of her work on our understandings of 'dirt' in the context of the growing body of literature that focuses on 'dirty work', i.e. work that is seen as disgusting or undesirable. Douglas advances an anthropological account which sees dirt as 'matter out of place' – an expression of symbolic systems in which dirt, by definition, is that which 'offends against order' (Douglas, 1966: 45). Cleanliness and dirt are accordingly not simply material matters but are typically imbued with a social and moral significance which, with respect to dirt, underpins a desire to avoid or remove it. We examine the influence of her work through the dominant emphasis in current accounts of dirty work on meanings attached to the work and on ideological strategies to manage taint. Finally, we discuss how recent literature has drawn on Douglas to take 'dirty work' in a different direction – one which is less concerned with looking at dirt as primarily a cultural category and which incorporates more explicitly its material dimensions.

Brief biography

Margaret Douglas was born in Italy in 1921. Her parents at the time were on their way home from Burma, where her father served in the Indian Civil Service. Together with her younger sister, and with both her parents abroad, she spent her early years with her maternal grandparents in Devon. After the early death of her mother in 1933, and two years later her beloved grandfather, she was sent as a boarder to the Catholic Sacred Heart Convent in Roehampton, South West London. Against this background of loss, she found a sense of belonging and security in the order and regularity of the school, which Fardon (1999), one of the first to document her life, sees as foundational for her focus on the significance she subsequently attached to hierarchy and order in organizations. Her religious background and upbringing were also to have a profound influence on her work (she drew on the Old Testament in particular to support some of her ideas) and she remained a practising Catholic all her life.

In 1939 she went to war-time Oxford to attend St Anne's College, where she read Philosophy, Politics and Economics. On leaving Oxford, she worked at the British Colonial office where she met several social anthropologists – the start of a life-long interest in the area, and foundational in her subsequent academic career. She returned to Oxford in 1946 to study anthropology under Edward Evans-Pritchard, with whom she remained close friends until his death in 1973. A doctoral programme followed in 1949 and her research took her to what was then the Belgian Congo (now the Democratic Republic of Congo) where she studied the Lele tribe, a group of about 30,000 people living along the Kasai River. In 1950 she completed her doctorate and married James Douglas with whom she had three children: Janet, James and Philip. She taught at University College, London, where she remained for around 25 years, becoming Professor of Social Anthropology. During this time, she taught and wrote at several universities in the United States, publishing in areas of risk, ritual, consumption and welfare economics, returning to UCL in 1988.

Douglas's early work was shaped by her African ethnography and it was in the 1960s that, heavily influenced by Durkheim and the Durkheimian sociology of Evans-Pritchard, she published her celebrated book *Purity and Danger* (1966). Her analysis of ritual, purity and pollution in different societies and times is still considered a key text in social anthropology today. This was followed in 1970 by *Natural Symbols*, which linked features of institutional organizations with patterns of belief and morality; her conclusion that differentiated, hierarchical and bounded institutions provided the most conducive environments for complex thinking and symbolism remained central to much of her work. She died aged 86 in 2007 and is survived by her three children.

Broader perspectives

A key strand that runs through Douglas's work, which she developed over the length of her career and which spans diverse areas such as anthropology, political science, sociology, institutional economics, psychology and biblical studies, is an understanding of institutions and how they explain styles of human thought – where rather than 'floating free' in a post-structuralist sense, ideas are seen as closely tied to social context. From a causal, institutionalist perspective, her key argument is that forms of social organization shape and explain 'thought styles', namely, how people classify, remember, forget or feel, through everyday ritual enactment. Beliefs, and their consequences, are accordingly seen as a by-product of the dynamics of institutional ordering, for example, its hierarchies and social regulation. As 6 and Richards (2017) argue, this has provided the micro-foundations for 'one of the most promising theories of institutional dynamics available in the social sciences' which Douglas herself variously applied to the institutional economics of consumer choice, analysis of poverty in developmental studies, sociology of terrorism and the political science of environmental governance.

Drawing on Durkheim's (1912) distinction between mechanical solidarity (based on similarity) and organic solidarity (based on accommodation of difference), she outlined a taxonomy of four elementary forms of organization based on the strength or weakness of social integration and regulation – though she recognised the likelihood, empirically, for hybrid arrangements. First outlined in *Natural Symbols* (Douglas, 1970), these forms are: 'hierarchy' (strong regulation and integration); 'individualism' (weak regulation and integration); 'enclave' (weak regulation, strong integration); and 'isolate ordering' (strong regulation, weak integration) – comprising a methodological 'template' for the comparative analysis that formed the basis of much of her work. These forms of social organization, characterised by the levels of social regulation and social integration of their informal institutions as above, shape and specify organization and thought style in any setting and scale. In their succinct commentary and analysis of her work, 6 and Richards explain that these forms capture 'how rigidly people treat their classifications, how flexibly they accommodate fallback options, how far they are prepared to contemplate compromise, how they conceive of the past and the future, how they deal with things anomalous within their implicit schemes for classifying problems and opportunities, and what emotions they attach to their beliefs' (6 and Richards, 2017: 10). We can see within her framework and her typology of social forms a high level of order which, as Fardon (1999) points out, may be symptomatic of the value she placed on order and security during her early years – a security she found, as referred to earlier, within the regularity and stable hierarchies of her boarding school.

Drawing on her doctoral research, Douglas argues that these thought styles are cultivated through day-to-day, small scale performative ritual where classification, symbolization, meanings and anomaly are central, and where individuals, in their classification systems and the rituals that support them, display a drive for consistency. People accordingly ritually perform their social organization in all its forms (Douglas, 1982) and it is through ritual that styles of thought are created and maintained. In other words, people enact and perform the strength of the social integration and social regulation of their social organization, thereby training and shaping patterns of thought – which in turn reinforce the social organization. The 'feedback loop', however, starts with social organization.

This provides a functionalist, causal explanation for aspects of human behaviour and here she had a particular focus on conflict. She suggests that, having been cultivated by forms of organization with their own particular hierarchies and social ordering, ritual may lead others to assert their own or others' interests in reaction through, for example, clashes with adjacent hierarchies or groups, leading in turn to rituals of conflict containment. Elementary forms therefore contain dynamics of both reinforcement, and resistance or reaction – thinking she applied in her later work to terrorist enclaves (see Douglas and Mars, 2003).

Douglas's work on forms of organization has engendered critique (e.g. Skorupski, 1979) on the grounds that she has not provided sufficient empirical justification for her claims – though as 6 and Richards (2017) suggests, this may have reflected a reluctance at the time to accept ethnography as sufficient in terms of empirical research. A more substantial critique concerns her focus on context as the driving force behind thought processes and ritual enactments, which has been interpreted as overly relativist (see Fardon, 1999 for a full discussion) due to her emphasis on the social determination of thought. In response, she pointed out that relativism is itself a thought style that is linked to social context, requiring explanation with reference to the social organization that has brought it about.

Purity and danger

From the above, we can see that from Douglas's perspective, classifications are part of a prevailing system of thought, reflecting a cognitive drive for consistency and order. These inevitably produce anomalies which are treated differently in different societies. It is these anomalies that should form the basis of research, particularly in terms of how they are explained and managed, i.e. in terms of the social organization that generated them. While the strategies to deal with anomalies may vary, she suggested that they routinely provoke disquiet, either through associations with notions of pollution or danger – and it was this fundamental, namely, the role of anomalies in understandings of dirt and of pollution, that formed the basis for her book *Purity and Danger.*

Purity and Danger is undoubtedly Douglas's best known work. Described by Fardon (1999) as a 'modern masterpiece', it has not been out of print since its publication in 1966 and has been translated into several languages. Its distinctiveness not only lies in how she drew on cognitive sciences (through the drive to understand the world through order and classification) to theorise how the human mind responds to categorical anomalies, but also in terms of its dialogue with both religious studies and the arts (Duschinsky, 2013; 2016). The reviews of the book at the time were, however, 'lukewarm', with one describing it rather condescendingly as 'lively' but not 'novel' and another claiming that social anthropologists would 'gain little' in the way of substantive knowledge (see Fardon, 1999). Others have more recently argued that there are a multiplicity of forms of classification (Valeri, 1999) and that order, rather than being stable as she assumes, is in fact fluid and uncertain (Hetherington and Lee, 2000) – a point that Douglas acknowledges in her later work where she recognises that society is not necessarily a unitary whole (Douglas, 2005).

Highlighting what she saw as an unjustified division between 'primitive' and 'modern' thinking, and following the section above, she argued in *Purity and Danger* that how we see the world depends, cognitively, on the deployment of prior categories and classifications which reflect the system of societal organization. These are moulded and sustained by social forces of ritual action and the deployment of symbols. Drawing on her structural approach, she explains: 'no particular set of classifying symbols can be understood in isolation, but there can be hope of making sense of them in relation to the total structure of classifications in the culture in question' (Douglas, 1966: vii). However, some instances may defy classification, such as meanings that can be classified in two or more rival ways, highlighting the role of contestation and conflict in the creation and sustaining of anomalies. How anomalies are managed will depend on the nature of the social organization concerned: they may be celebrated, suppressed as dangerous or evil, or special institutions may develop to treat them as exceptions to be controlled. Referring to Durkheim's dichotomy, she suggests that societies based on mechanical solidarity are likely to debar anomalies and those based on organic solidarity are more likely to lend themselves to accommodating such difference.

It is this thinking about the role of anomalies that lies behind her now celebrated definition of dirt as 'disorder', as 'matter out of place' and 'in the eye of the beholder' (a form of thinking that she claimed emanated from observing how her husband's 'threshold of tolerance' of dirt differed from her own – though she did not specify the direction). With shades, again, of her Catholic girlhood, if cleanliness is order, where classification systems remain 'intact', dirt and pollution are accordingly disorder and a violation of those systems: 'Dirt offends against order. Eliminating it is not a negative movement but a positive effort to organize the environment' (Douglas, 1966: 2). In other words, eliminating dirt is not a material matter, based for example on anxiety to escape disease, but involves a positive re-ordering that is an attempt to create a unity of experience, a point of contention that has been picked up by different scholars (Rozin et al., 2000 for example have argued that a disease avoidance mechanism may accompany cultural and moral values, i.e. that both can co-exist). Douglas contends that these rituals of purity and impurity create unity where symbolic patterns are worked out and publicly displayed.

Seeing dirt as 'matter out of place' therefore implies two conditions: firstly, a set of ordered relations and secondly a contravention of that order. Dirt is never a unique, isolated phenomenon but is part of a system – the by-product of a 'systematic ordering and classification of matter' (Douglas, 1966: 35) where ordering inevitably involves the rejection of inappropriate elements. Disorder is destructive of existing patterns and from this perspective symbolises both danger and power. Dirt, as she puts it, is relative and takes us into the field of symbolism and symbolic systems of purity. Thus, food is not inherently dirty but food bespattered on clothing or spilt on a table cloth is seen as such. In other words, our 'pollution behavior is the reaction which condemns any object or idea likely to confuse or contradict cherished classifications' (Douglas, 1966: 36), a tendency she locates in psychological preferences for perceiving and recognising patterns or schema which, once labelled, become sedimented in cultural categories and afforded authority. These anomalies serve to strengthen our belief in the main or primary classification but overall, uncleanliness or dirt is 'that which must not be included if a pattern is to be maintained'. Dirt is accordingly a form of anomaly.

To illustrate, she draws on Jewish dietary laws (the ban on pork and the perceived 'uncleanliness' of pigs) as set out in the Book of Leviticus and how these laws should be seen as an 'aide-memoire' (6 and Richards, 2017) for the way in which society is organized and not a reflection of any inherent 'dirtiness'. These prohibitions form part of social system of rationalization for particular boundaries, classifications and structures. In this respect, unclean animals are anomalous and this is the main reason they are outcast as forbidden. The pig is cloven-hoofed but not ruminant and this transgresses an existing classification which combines the two. In other words, species are unclean which are 'imperfect members of their class, or whose class itself confounds the general scheme of the world' (Douglas, 1966: 55), incompatible with holiness and with blessing. Anomaly therefore only makes sense within a system of classification which in turn reflects the system of societal organization. Here, ritual addresses this potency for disorder and 'undefinability'. For example, as she illustrates, the Lele regard the unborn child, with its ambiguous position in terms of its gender and its ability to survive, as potentially dangerous to others through an assumed malevolence, so the mother must maintain distance from those who are vulnerable or ill. Danger (and hence pollution) therefore lies in transitional states (neither one thing nor the other) and this danger is controlled by ritual. In the caste system, one's place in the hierarchy of purity is biologically transmitted through the mother, so sexual behaviour is carefully patrolled to preserve the purity of caste – particularly the behaviour of women – expressive of a desire to keep the body physical and the body social intact. Pollution ideas are enlisted to bind men and women in their allotted roles within a social system.

Ambiguities in the classification systems therefore engender anomalies that are seen as dangerous or polluting and rituals of cleansing are used to recover purity and ward off dangers of dirt and/or pollutants. While these rituals were largely religiously inspired in more 'primitive' cultures, in the modern world classifications still exist and are underscored by different systems of knowledge and action – such as around sexuality, environmental pollution, corruption and scandal – so that each culture has its own notion of dirt and defilement that is part of a larger whole in its social system.

From purity and danger to dirty work

Mary Douglas's work on the symbolic dimensions of dirt has had a profound influence on the burgeoning literature on dirty work in the sociology of work and in organization studies. While this literature does not necessarily share her structuralist tendencies insofar as she sees meanings as rooted in social systems, it has adopted in the main her orientation to dirt as 'disorder' and as 'matter out of place'. This literature has largely adopted a socially constructionist perspective which, informed by *Purity and Danger*, perceives dirt in relative terms – as 'in the eyes of the beholder', subject to particular perceptions and contingencies rather than containing any 'essential' quality. In other words, as J. Hughes et al. (2016) and others have pointed out, this focuses on the meanings afforded to dirt based on different perceptions of how it has, from Douglas's point of view, 'violated' a cultural order, rather than on the possession of any essential attribute. With clear reference to Douglas, Ashforth and Kreiner summarise the approach to dirty work thus:

> "Dirtiness" is a social construction: it is not inherent in the work itself or the workers but is imputed by people, based on necessarily subjective standards of cleanliness and purity ... the common denominator among tainted jobs is not so much their specific attributes but the visceral repugnance of people to them.
>
> (Ashforth and Kreiner, 1999: 415)

The sociological significance of dirt therefore lies in how dirt is perceived by others, where society 'equates cleanliness with goodness and dirt with badness' (Ashforth and Kreiner, 1999: 416). Everett Hughes (1958), one of the first to consider dirty work in his book *Men and their Work*, elaborates the connection between dirt as a physical and as a moral category: 'It may be simply physically disgusting. It may be a symbol of degradation, something that wounds one's dignity' (Hughes 1958: 49). On this basis, there is a 'moral division of labour' in that some people are able to avoid dealing with dirt and can get others to do the 'dirt work' on their behalf, stigmatising those involved. Cleanliness and dirt therefore are seen as having a social and moral significance with avoidance rules often meaning that work dealing with physical dirt is carried out by those who occupy lesser positions in the social hierarchy, with implications for prestige, work hierarchies and social positioning.

These social and moral dimensions were developed by Ashforth and Kreiner (1999) in an article published in the *Academy of Management Review*, one of the first to consider dirty work in a contemporary context in terms of how it is encountered and experienced. Drawing on E. Hughes (1958) above, they present a typology of dirty work that has become foundational for much of the work in the field. Here, they refer to Douglas's definition of dirt and delineate three forms of taint based on different occupations or roles: physical taint, which covers work that is associated with dirt or danger such as refuse collectors or miners; social taint, which relates to work that involves regular contact with people from stigmatised groups and/or which is seen as servile to others such as prison officers or domestic cleaners; and moral taint, which refers to work that is regarded as sinful or of dubious virtue such as debt collectors or sex workers. However, while the concept of physical taint has potential to incorporate some of the physical dimensions of dirty work, the focus is still on this form of work's socially constructed nature through an emphasis on meanings and perceptions, from the perspective of 'the beholder', rather than on any intrinsic, physical dirtiness of the job.

As we have seen, the idea of dirt as a contravention of social order that transgresses particular boundaries means that those involved in dirty work can be stigmatised, morally and socially, through association so that individuals are 'tainted', making identity management problematic (Bolton, 2005; Dick, 2005). Bolton (2005) and others suggest that people are often aware of the stigma attached to their work, raising issues about how people manage job-related stigma. Ashforth and Kreiner (1999) identify various 'normalization' strategies that involve processes of meaning making that help workers present the job as 'acceptable' and 'ordinary' (see also Ashforth et al., 2007), enhancing how it is perceived. Workers collectively 'make sense' of their occupation in terms its importance and significance, where this sense making is typically anchored in wider meanings about what is socially valued. Some research, for example, has highlighted how demonstrating mastery of the dirtiest aspects of the job can be a source of value. Thus, care workers can find a sense of distinctiveness, pride and moral authority in the ability to undertake work that others would be too 'squeamish' to perform (Stacey, 2005). Bolton (2005) highlights how gynaecology nurses take pride in dealing with unpleasant aspects of their work that involve intimate, bodily care; J. Hughes et al. (2016) refer to how refuse collectors gain satisfaction from doing an essential service under difficult conditions and how this engenders a strong occupational and workgroup culture; while Johnson and Hodge (2014) similarly describe how members of a security team deflect taint by placing emphasis on their resilience and their emotional detachment when dealing with dangerous tasks.

These different ideological strategies have been conceptualised by Ashforth and Kreiner (1999) under three key headings, all oriented towards the need to recast dirty work in affirmative terms. These strategies include: 'reframing' the meaning of dirty work by infusing it with positive value (e.g. seeing such work as a badge of honour or a mission); 'recalibrating', that is adjusting the perceptual and evaluative standards used to assess the work and thereby minimising the 'dirty work' component (e.g. hospital cleaners may introduce notions of patient care as integral to the work); and 'refocusing' through the shifting of attention away from the stigmatised to the non-stigmatised features of the job (e.g. refuse collectors may focus on the benefits of social solidarity and of working outside) – a typology that has formed the basis of many empirical studies in the area. Following Douglas, the emphasis in the dirty work literature therefore has been on a view of dirt as a symbolic and cultural category and on strategies of 'meaning making' that are tied to the values of a social system, in order to deal with stigma at work. On this basis, we can see through perceptions of the relativity of dirt and the significance of different meanings attached to it, the ongoing influence of *Purity and Danger* in current accounts of dirty work.

Moving on from *Purity and Danger*

In order to illustrate the significance of anomalies in classification, Douglas draws on Sartre's essay on stickiness and slime. She sees slime as anomalous because it confounds a cultural classification based on liquidity versus solidity: it is neither one thing nor the other and it is this ambiguity that we find unsettling. However, Sartre argues that viscosity, in the form of slime, repels in its own right as a primary, phenomenal experience. While Douglas sees slime as primarily a cultural phenomenon that challenges classifications, for Sartre the ambiguity of slime also lies in its anomalous materiality, for example, how it feels on the skin. Therefore, our response to slime is not just cultural and relative but is based on material, embodied experience. As Dant and Bowles (2003) argue, one can extrapolate from this understanding of slime to other forms of dirt whereby 'ambiguous materials' cling to surfaces such as the skin and which, through touch and smell, elicit an embodied response. This provides a phenomenological underpinning to the idea of dirt as 'matter out of place' – one which signifies a 'fundamental relation' with our own being but which may get 'overlaid' with cultural significance over time causing us to revalue what counts as dirt and dirtiness. In other words, while Douglas argues for the primacy of the cultural in understandings of dirt, Dant and Bowles see a cotermineity with its material, embodied dimensions. Dirt is not always an expression of a symbolic system but has practical and 'rational' considerations as well as rituals and moral codes.

In this respect, her work has not only had a direct influence on socially constructed understandings of dirt and dirty work dominant in the field – understandings that foreground dirt's contingent and relational dimensions – but has also, as a point of departure and in a counter-positional sense, helped to lay the foundations for a more material and embodied account. These emerging accounts go beyond the meanings and cultural significance attached to dirt and dirty work (e.g. through ideological constructions and responses that give the work positive value) to include its material dimensions.

Thus Dant and Bowles (2003) above draw heavily on Douglas's work to present an account of car repair work that foregrounds the practical problems of dealing with oil and grease, showing how responses to dirt are not always ritualistic or ideological in form, as Douglas supposed, but are governed by pragmatics (e.g. the need to keep dirt away from the precision-engineered machinery; the potential for dirt to compromise personal health and safety). Durr and Winder (2016) take Douglas's understanding of purity and pollution as a point of departure to understand social hierarchies and inequalities in urban space. Looking at Mexico City, they argue that both physical and symbolic dimensions of dirt need to be considered to understand how they come together to form socio-material assemblages, shaped by power dynamics and embodied movement. As they show, the materiality of garbage matters, provoking emotional engagements as well as conflict through the entanglement of the material with the human.

Similarly, J. Hughes et al. (2016), through a study of refuse collectors and street cleaners, demonstrate how workers see dirt in both relative *and* absolute terms. Thus, following Douglas and in terms of the former, waste and debris that lay within the boundaries of acceptability (e.g. matter that was appropriately bagged and disposed of) were not always seen as dirty but were 'normalised' and integrated into valued notions of 'doing an essential service', seen as part of the work's routines. Dirt was largely seen as waste and debris that was 'disorderly' or 'out of place' – inappropriately bagged or put in the wrong container. Thus, leaf-cuttings dropped onto a just-swept street or metal objects put in the container for wood were seen as dirt and the perpetrators as 'dirty people', highlighting the contingent nature of dirt and its relative properties. By the same token, however, there was a substantive element to dirt and its experience. Some forms of matter were always dirty and could not be ideologically reframed or incorporated into an 'essential' service. Rotting food, used cat litter or excrement, put out in flimsy bags as waste for the collection team, could leave streaks and slimy substances on clothes and skin, eliciting disgust through touch and smell and potentially interfering with positive, ideological constructions around the work. Equally, Simpson et al. (2014), in a study of the butcher trade, show how blood and gore can lodge under finger nails and stain clothing – a potential source of contamination that requires formalised practices of removal: the careful washing of hands; the cleaning and sterilization of equipment that hands or raw meat have touched. While these practices may be, as Douglas suggests, ritualised if only to the extent that they are based in part on repetitive behaviours, they are also grounded in the pragmatics and physical principles of hygiene and the avoidance of contamination. This suggests that cultural meanings alone may not be sufficient to explain and understand the experiences of those working with dirt and that its materiality has a fundamental influence.

Conclusion

In this chapter we have explored some of the contributions of the acclaimed social anthropologist, Mary Douglas, to understandings of work and organization through her foundational text, *Purity and Danger*. For Douglas, purity and impurity discourses are not confined to 'primitive' cultures or societies, as was orthodox at the time, but play important boundary drawing roles in all human societies and systems of organization. We have shown the influence of her work through a dominant, relativist understanding of dirt as disorder and as matter out of place within the literature on dirty work as well as some of the boundaries constructed around dirt's proximity – boundaries that are managed through various forms of socially informed meaning making. At the same time, we have demonstrated the influence of her work, in a counter-positional sense, through a more material understanding of occupations dealing with dirt that takes *Purity and Danger* as a point of departure. While this work may not share her structuralist approach, which links categorical systems to social structure, and while the literature may place varying levels of emphasis on the symbolic, it highlights in different ways the significance of social divisions associated with dirt and the role of dirt as a social, physical and moral entity.

Following the above, Douglas's work and the themes of purity and impurity form the foundations, potentially, for a rich trajectory in terms of future research. This could explore different, emerging cultural practices of 'ritual purity' in organizations and how they 'inflect' modern, contextually driven notions of conformity, morality and transgression. For example, managerialist practices of performance management and review based on 'purist' neo-liberal ideologies and reasoning, may be positioned as an attempt to impose order on an inherently 'untidy' experience, with (often ritualised) sanctions imposed on those who fail to meet the standards required. Examination of other work-based rituals (board-room formalities, management processes, team meetings, coffee breaks, business lunches, norms and practices of communication), as well as of new manifestations of work-based stigma ('uncaring' public officials, 'greedy' bankers, perpetrators of discriminatory or oppressive practices), opens up new conversations and new understandings of hierarchies, order, control, complicity and transgression. Such an examination may encompass how appeals to and images of purity and impurity shape the organizational subject as well as how they form the basis for organizational and wider discourses such as those around morality, inequality and fairness; how organizations incorporate anomalies and contradictions such as when managerialist practices collide with wider notions of the 'common good'; and, from our earlier account, how physical and symbolic dimensions of dirt and pollution can come together to forge a deeper, more embodied understanding of work-based subjectivity and experience. *Purity and Danger* can accordingly be seen to have an enduring influence in terms of how we may, through notions of purity, cleanliness, pollution and dirt, 'read' the culture of organizations and some of the microprocesses such organizations contain.

Recommended reading

Original text by Mary Douglas

Douglas, M. (1966) *Purity and Danger: Analysis of the Concepts of Pollution and Taboo*. London: Routledge and Kegan Paul.

Key academic text

Duschinsky, R. (2013) The Politics of Purity: When, Actually, Is Dirt Matter Out of Place?, *Thesis Eleven*, 119(1): 63–77.

Accessible resource

6 P. and Richards, P. (2017) *Mary Douglas: Understanding Social Thought and Conflict*, New York/Oxford: Berghahn.

References

Ashforth, B. and Kreiner, G. (1999) "How Can You Do It?" Dirty Work and the Challenge of Constructing a Positive Identity, *Academy of Management Review*, 24(3): 413–434.

Ashforth, B., Kreiner, G., Clark, M. and Fugate, M. (2007) Normalizing Dirty Work: Managerial Tactics for Countering Occupational Taint, *Academy of Management Journal*, 50(1): 149–174.

Bolton, S. (2005) Women's Work, Dirty Work: The Gynaecology Nurse as Other, *Gender Work and Organization*, 12(2): 169–186.

Dant, T. and Bowles, D. (2003) Dealing with Dirt: Servicing and Repairing Cars, *Sociological Research Online*, 8(2): 1–17. www.socresonline.org.uk/8/2/dant.html

Dick, P. (2005) Dirty Work Designations: How Police Officers Account for Their Use of Coercive Force, *Human Relations*, 58(11): 1363–1390.

Douglas, M. (1966) *Purity and Danger: Analysis of the Concepts of Pollution and Taboo*, London: Routledge and Kegan Paul.

Douglas, M. (1970) *Natural Symbols: Explorations in Cosmology*, London: Routledge.

Douglas, M. (1982[1978]) Cultural Bias. In: *In the Active Voice*, London: Routledge and Kegan Paul, 183–254.

Douglas, M. (2005) A Feeling for Hierarchy. In: *Believing Scholars*, J. Heft (ed.), New York: Fordham University Press, 94–120.

Douglas, M. and Mars, G. (2003) Terrorism: A Positive Feedback Game, *Human Relations*, 56(7): 763–786.

Durkheim, E. (1995[1912]) *The Elementary Forms of Religious Life*, K. Fields (Trans), New York: Free Press.

Dürr, E. and Winder, G. (2016) Garbage at work: Ethics, subjectivation and resistance in Mexico. In: *Purity and Danger Now: New Perspectives*, R. Duschinsky, S. Schnall and D. Weiss (eds), London and New York: Routledge, 52–68.

Duschinsky, R. (2013) The Politics of Purity: When, Actually, is Dirt Matter Out of Place?, *Thesis Eleven*, 119(1): 63–77.

Duschinsky, R. (2016) Introduction. In: *Purity and Danger Now: New Perspectives*, R. Duschinsky, S. Schnall and D. Weiss (eds), Abingdon: Routledge, 24–85.

Fardon, R. (1999) *Mary Douglas: An Intellectual Biography*, London/New York: Routledge.

6 P. and Richards, P. (2017) *Mary Douglas: Understanding Social Thought and Conflict*, New York/Oxford: Berghahn.

Hetherington, K. and Lee, N. (2000) Social Order and the Blank Figure, *Environment and Planning D: Society and Space*, 18(2): 169–184.

Hughes, E. (1958) *Men and Their Work*, Glencoe, IL: Free Press.

Hughes, J., Simpson, R., Slutskaya, N., Simpson, A. and Hughes, K. (2016) Beyond the Symbolic: A Relational Approach to Dirty Work Through a Study of Refuse Collectors and Street Cleaners, *Work, Employment and Society*, 31(1): 106–122.

Johnston, M. and Hodge, E. (2014) Dirt, Death and Danger? I Don't Recall Any Adverse Reaction …': Masculinity and the Taint Management of Hospital Private Security Work, *Gender Work and Organization*, 21(6): 546–558.

Rozin, P., Haidt, J. and Clore, G. (2000) Disgust. In: *Handbook of Emotions*, 2nd edition, M. Lewis and J. Havilard-Hanes (eds), New York: Guilford Press, 637–653.

Simpson, R., Hughes, J., Slutskaya, N. and Balta, M. (2014) Sacrifice and Distinction in Dirty Work: Men's Construction of Meaning in the Butcher Trade, *Work, Employment and Society*, 28(5): 754–770.

Skorupski, J. (1979) 'Pangolin Power' and 'Our Philosopher Replies'. In: *Philosophical Disputes and the Social Sciences*, S.C. Brown (ed.), Sussex: Harvester Press.

Stacey, C. (2005) Finding Dignity in Dirty Work: The Constraints and Rewards of Low-Wage Home Care Labour, *Sociology of Health and Illness*, 27(6): 831–854.

Valeri, V. (1999) *The Forest of Taboos: Morality, Hunting and Identity Among the Huaulu of Moluccas*. Wisconsin: University of Wisconsin Press.

4 1984

Women scholars re-visioning organizational life

Amanda Sinclair

If, as feminism has posited, one deplorable tic of patriarchal sensibility is to over-abstractify, then surely one of the geniuses of women is ... to address the reader, directly, unpompously, and even intimately.

Robyn Morgan introducing Marilyn Waring's *Women, Politics and Power* (1985)

When I was considering contributing to this volume, I wasn't sure which women scholars to choose. Many in organizational studies qualified – had been foundational and pivotal to me – but were largely neglected in the male canon of organization and management theory. My decisions were made for me by two factors and determine the authors and texts I focus on in this chapter: Judi Marshall's *Women Managers* (1984); Arlie Hochschild's *The Managed Heart* (1983); and Kathy Ferguson's *The Feminist Case Against Bureaucracy* (1984).

First, I decided I wanted to do something different here: to describe these writers' contributions through their impact on me as a junior academic in the late 1980s and 1990s. While George Orwell famously prophesied a dystopian world in 1984, the early 1980s was a rich and fertile time for women scholars researching and writing about organizations and management. I remember vividly the relief, energy and freedom I felt reading the work of women from that period. Walking back across the Melbourne University campus with Judi Marshall's *Women Managers* tucked in my bag, I felt licensed to focus, think and write about subjects, and in ways that mattered to me! Differently but equally powerfully, I can still feel my stomach turning with the stark truth of Kathy Ferguson's thesis about bureaucracies and the urgency of a radical feminist critique. Reading *Feminist Critique* filled me with trepidation, left nowhere to hide. I couldn't remain complacent or complicit. Each authorised me through their examples to experiment in my own research and writing. Each 'body' of writing made me braver, giving voice to my own (also embodied) experiences as researcher, reader, writer.

The second factor that made my choice for me is the treasure trove that is my office bookshelf. Over the weeks following the invitation to write, I did what is a very odd thing these days and closed my laptop to spend time re-reading these books. I've got around four shelves of books covering issues of gender, feminism, masculinity and diversity. As a poorly-paid part-time lecturer, I bought few books, largely relying on the library instead. But there were a few I did purchase, read with excitement and recommended to students. When I looked at my bookshelf, there they were! A good number of these very influential books were published in the mid 1980s. I contacted my own publisher, Allen & Unwin, to congratulate them – they'd published many of these, often revolutionary, feminist books. Who was the visionary publisher back then, I wondered? I found pencil scribbles and page numbers with asterisks and comments noted in the backs of each of these books which mapped 'brilliant' and 'best bits' for me when I first read them in the late 1980s. Jotted alongside page numbers were titles of articles I was working on, showing how they inspired and provoked my teaching and published work over the next decades (for example Sinclair, 1992, 1994, 1998).

Me and the wider context

In the late 1980s I was relatively new to the management and organizational field having done my PhD in a Politics department. I joined the Melbourne Business School in 1988 as a part-time lecturer and set about trying to get my doctoral work published. I'd undertaken a longitudinal study of senior management teams, critiquing the contemporary management infatuation with teams to 'fix' complex problems. It eventually appeared – after several rejections – in a 1992 issue of *Organization Studies* as 'The Tyranny of a Team Ideology'. I was hungry for critical perspectives on organizations. But I wanted ones that were readable, and that modelled how to be a different kind of organizational scholar myself, including how to write critically but engagingly.

Although I focus here on three organizational researchers because of their particular impact on me, they stood within a wider tsunami (I was going to say 'blossoming' but opted for a less tame noun!) of 1980s feminist and women's writing. Many of these writers were not organizational scholars, but they offered radical, relevant commentary on gender, power and institutions, on hegemonic masculinist methods of knowledge-making and research production. They pointed to women's (often unregistered or excluded) experiences in public and organizational life. Among the many I thirstily drank were: Jean Baker Miller (1976); Carol Gilligan (1982); Hester Eisenstein (1984); Marilyn Waring (1985, 1988), with her devastating and much under-valued critique of economics and public policy tools;

Mary Belenky and her colleagues in *Women's Ways of Knowing* (1986); Sandra Harding's *Feminism and Methodology* (1987); and Rosemary Pringle's fantastic *Secretaries Talk* (1988).

A few years later when I was teaching MBA students Management and Ethics, I drew on Miller, Gilligan and Belenky to subvert the patri-archal canon parading as the 'Business Ethics' literature. I have slides of Gilligan's ethics of care, the implications of which I insisted we discuss in class! These authors also prompted me to problematise MBA classrooms, how structures, teaching and learning methods often excluded women and devalued their diverse experiences and understandings (Sinclair, 1995, 1997). I set about trying to explore and create more inclusive, enlivening and transformative classroom environments and model a different kind of embodied pedagogy myself (see also hooks, 1984). It's a project that I am still engaged in.

As one of only two women in the Business School during this period (and both of us at the bottom of the hierarchy), I sought out and was sup-ported by feminist academics in other faculties, such as psychologist Norma Grieve and history professor Patricia Grimshaw, who co-edited a series of multi-disciplinary volumes applying feminist methods to a wide range of public policy and other contemporary topics (for example, 1981). They prompted me to read more widely in feminist analyses, for example film and cultural theorists such as Barbara Creed (also a Melbourne academic), as well as feminist critiques of psychology, social psychology and research methods that were being published at this time.

To better theorise and understand organizations with their self-reproduc-ing management and leadership cultures, this broader feminist scholarship was very helpful to me. For example, it provided resonant explanations of the allure of heroic, muscular archetypes of leadership, as well as why soci-eties feel deep unease with women in charge (Sinclair, 1994; 1998). It was also written differently. It didn't have the effect of making me feel a dummy or an outsider, which some other work by critical organizational scholars did. Reading these writers taught me how valuable it is to read widely, to look at organizational phenomena from other disciplinary perspectives, and to learn from feminist methods and their critiques of conventional research practice. They also taught me to write with the reader in mind: to see them as partners, as my colleague Christine Nixon would say, not as pupils in need of instruction.

I live in Australia and it is probably not coincidental that the late 1970s and early 1980s saw second wave feminism gain particular traction in Australian politics and in bureaucracies with the rise of the 'femocrat'. Australian governments were pioneers in equal opportunity and affirma-tive action reforms. Indeed, Hester Eisenstein used her reflections about working in Australia versus the United States as the title of her book *Gender Shock: practising feminisms on two continents* (1991).

I was also receptive! In the mid 1980s, I had just finished my PhD and had started a new research project interviewing feminists in local government. At a personal level, my first marriage had just ended and I had two young children. I had few resources and little time but was hungry for authors writing about phenomena that were recognisable to me and helped me make sense of my own – very difficult at this time – experiences.

I have written this chapter from a personal perspective to capture the embodied way in which I was nourished by all these authors, but especially Judi Marshall, Kathy Ferguson and Arlie Hochschild. Finding, reading and feeling sometimes empowered, sometimes confronted, by the writing of each was as much a physical feeling as an intellectual one (Sinclair and Ladkin, 2018). They drove me to be braver and bolder about naming the gendered regimes of which I was a part (Sinclair, 1995). Their research changed me: the things I attended to; how I went about research, theorising and writing; what kind of academic I became.

Reading back over their work I am dazzled by the originality and freshness of the ideas and scholarship I discuss here. I have also consulted some of their recent writing, for example Arlie Hochschild's *Strangers in Their Own Land* (2016) and Judi Marshall's *First Person Action Research: Living Life as Inquiry* (2016), to enjoy them, but also to get a sense of and to convey the bigger sweep of their contribution over more than three decades.

Writing women's experiences of management – Judi Marshall

> Judi Marshall opens her *Women Managers* book with "the backcloth to my writing is fertile chaos. The book emerges out of conflicts and contradictions. These appear both in the public arena ... and in the personal lives of many women"
>
> (1984: 1)

In teasing out the setting of 'fertile chaos', Judi spends a good part of this introduction, and indeed the book, locating herself, her shifts and choices as a management writer who is also a woman. She continues

> my aim is to identify key issues, and explore the options ... It will soon become apparent that this is definitely not a "How to" (make it in management) book. It is rather a "What do you want?" and "Who are you?" book.
>
> (ibid)

I can't tell you how refreshing I found these words when I first read them. I still find them understated yet compelling – hallmarks of Judi Marshall's writing. I found *Women Managers* on the recommendation of an academic who had been the first woman teacher at Melbourne Business School. She left before I started – scarred by the experience. We ran into each other at an event. I got the sense she didn't think much of me or my prospects for having an impact on the business school culture. It was thrown out as a kind of afterthought: 'Have you read Judi Marshall's *Women Managers*?' Yet it was a fantastic recommendation in what was feeling like a barren landscape of writing about management. It was unlike anything else I'd read in the management space and, in its own unassuming way, seemed a revolutionary book.

Two particular features of *Women Managers* have been very influential in my own work. The first was the writing itself. It included, sometimes as quoted above in the opening statements, an honest and reflective account by the author of her shifting interest in the subject matter and its impact on her. Marshall admits she was a reluctant researcher in the 'women and management' space (see also Calas and Smircich, 1992; 1993). Like me, she was advised by male bosses and mentors that gender research was dangerous or 'career limiting'. She describes the recognition that she had 'submerged any awareness of being a woman, especially at work, and generally hoped to be treated as a person first' (1984: 5). She documents her surprise at finding out her sex had been significant to, noticed by, others.

Marshall then sets about charting her course to a feminist perspective. The second way her work has been powerful for me is the way it puts women and their experiences at the heart of her research. 'Women bring their femaleness, with its connotations and status in society, with them when they enter organizations' (1984: 4). Could I dare hope – not idealistically but practically – that listening to women would offer an alternative view of how we organize and conduct ourselves in management? Acknowledging the well-charted problems in taking the view that women managers might bring different emphases to management, such as essentialising and imposing a false unity on women, Marshall strikes out in this direction anyway. She offers, for example, a re-visioning of theories and concepts of power, noting that personal sources of power available to women include 'stamina, resilience, abilities to undergo change and regeneration and intuition based on understanding others' (1984: 110). Drawing on her sensitive, in-depth explorations with women managers, Judi urges other women facing obstacles to articulate and value characteristics and possibilities – such as co-operation and intuition – largely absent from dominant formulations of management (see also Marshall, 1995 for a moving analysis of how women managers 'move on' from conventional careers).

While all Marshall's analysis in *Women Managers* was helpful, it was the final pages headed 'Re-vision: Alternative futures' that provided a source from which I drank with relief – and then continued to drink – as my research on leadership, gender and sexualities unfolded for the next three decades, including my recent collaborative book with colleague and former Victorian Police Commissioner, Christine Nixon, *Women Leading* (2017) (see also 1995, 2002). Judi asks herself 'what the manager who draws on her female characteristics and culture at work faces' (1984: 229). She encourages a consciousness of ourselves as women, and urges us to develop our powers of speaking out and saying: 'it is different for women, and this is what it is like'.

I can't remember exactly how I came to visit Judi. I think I may have written to her and she invited me to the University of Bath. She understood that this would need to be *en famille*, with partner, children and baby in tow. I felt valued on that visit. Judi endorsed and encouraged me to teach to her groups the research on masculinities that I had undertaken and reported in my *Trials at the Top* (1994). I had enjoyed writing that little book of just 44 pages, which – just as I hoped – a male colleague told me he read on his tram ride to work. Short but, I hoped, punchy! It had a painting on the cover of Odysseus, tied to his mast being seduced by the sirens (the only one of my books that had a cover I loved). *Trials* was my first published effort to invite men and women to a readable account of the impact of masculinities in leadership. Judi referenced that book of mine in her work and offered the opportunity to share my research with her mature age students, men and women managers, some of whom stayed in touch with me.

These experiences began a career-long interest in doing and writing research in ways that could be shared with managers in organizations, with an interest in change – even emancipation, if that's not too big a word – from traditional practices. I have no interest in critical theory that stays obscure and unread by people in organizations. And I have only grown more impatient with the norms of academic journal writing that condemn us to reproducing painful conformist prose (see also Grey and Sinclair, 2006). Judi was key to showing me you could write important feminist books that were readable and impactful but also open and anchored in personal experience.

Emotions, emotional labour and writing with emotion

Arlie Hochschild's *The Managed Heart: Commercialization of Human Feeling* introduced me to the role emotions and 'feeling rules' play in organizations and leadership. Explorations of emotion and emotional labour were to become key themes in organizational studies over the 1980s and 1990s, but in my view Hochschild's book remains one of the most perceptive and beautifully, but lightly, theorised case studies. She was in the vanguard of those offering a critical view of emotions in organizations, showing that the delivery of feelings was often transacted under duress with unconscious but potentially damaging effects. Emotional displays obeyed gendered rules, that is, patience and care is required from women with little power as part of their roles. These rules are determined by higher status, male management to whom they do not apply.

Re-reading this 1983 book I am dazzled by how contemporary it feels. Its insights are as fresh and relevant today as they were when I first read them, perhaps more so because so many managerial, technical and ethical barriers to commercialising feelings and intimacy have been rolled back. Hochschild argues that emotions and feelings are always being produced in interaction with others. Yet there are latent 'feeling rules' that govern what is expected and owed in organizational feeling currencies. While these processes are as old as human interaction, what is new is the instrumental stance that is viewed as good management and effective customer service, of engineering feelings, along gender, class and power lines. Hochschild's research of airline attendants finds that delivering mandated feelings in organizational interactions 'affects the degree to which we listen to feeling and sometimes our very capacity to feel' (1983: 21). Her analysis opened up to scholars a new seam of de-humanising organizational practices, and ones which were widely seen and emulated as part of effective service delivery.

A second reason for the book's impact on me was that gender analysis was explicit. It wasn't incidental that most of the emotional displays that were being commanded and delivered – often at a personal cost – were by women, and most of the people in charge of commercialising and receiving that performance were male managers and customers. Hochschild maps how advertising, training, disciplining and remuneration were skewed to exploit gender stereotypes and perpetuate systemic gender inequalities.

She also interweaves through her account of these gendered organizational processes, hair-raising data and information about the regulation of bodies and sexualities and the impact of this on flight attendants. One of the airlines she studied promised customers 'we really move our tails for you to make your every wish come true' (1983: 93). Women were weighed before flights and even in some cases had thighs measured. Their weight was monitored and if it didn't go down to acceptable levels, disciplinary action was commenced. Appallingly behaved, harassing customers were labelled as 'mishandled', while flight attendants were held responsible and penalised for delivering inauthentic smiles and care.

In *The Managed Heart*, we hear the flight attendants joking and confiding, angry and exasperated, feeling powerless and plotting resistance, subversion and revolt. They become experts in non-payment of expected feelings and sexual withdrawal, protesting the overextension and over-use of the traditional feminine sexuality expected. They upend food trays on customers and use other tactics to defy trainers and evaluation systems. While we as readers cheer on these efforts, Hochschild also fearlessly probes the cost of this exploitation. Cabin crew become estranged from their own feelings, unable to re-connect in personal relationships, sometimes unable to summon feeling in their own sexual and wider lives.

At a theoretical level, this research provides a basis to dig more deeply and critically into patterns that management prescriptions often lionise. It was foundational for mainstream and gender researchers exploring dimensions of aesthetic, intimate and sexualised labour (for example Bolton, 2005; McMurray and Ward, 2014; Hancock et.al., 2015).

In my own case, I went on to explore issues of emotion, leadership identity and identity work, such as suppressing personal issues as weakness and working excessive hours, in *Trials at the Top* and *Doing Leadership Differently*. In my teaching and executive education I share Hochschild's findings and concepts included in later books such as *The Time Bind* (1997) and *Strangers in Their Own Land* (2016). For example, her research shows that as we put more hours and effort into work, home life becomes barren. Our families, friends, even pets, give up on us. She also documents the 'Taylorization' of intimate relationships where we schedule in 'relationship time' like an Outlook calendar:

8.10 pm: phone conversation with mother/mother in law
8.30 pm: talk to teenager
9.00 pm: ask partner how their day was. Negotiate when next to have sex so a row – and withdrawal of household support – is avoided

Relationships become transactional and the people on the other end know they are being ticked off our 'To Do' lists. As these encounters become emptied, we reinvest in work where people want to talk to us. Our sense of value and importance is reinforced.

In my experience, all managers recognise these patterns. Some believe they have no choice. Most also see it as a deal with the devil they are doing, sometimes rationalised as just for a time or through this difficult work patch. Our discussion in class of these patterns enables us to observe and question leadership identity processes, which has been one of the aims of my leadership development work with students and executives (Sinclair, 2007; 2011; 2013). At a personal level this research has helped me also open more bravely the doorway into my own leadership identity work, observing the ways I get sucked into performing myself as an academic and leader, a performance of which I can probably let go (Sinclair, 2004; 2010).

A third reason why Hochschild had such an impact on me is the way she writes and how, as a reader, I felt the courage and passion for change she brings to the issues she studies. She made research of stewards in the airline industry and their performance of emotion a phenomenon that non-academics, inhabitants of organizations, could recognise, care about, resist and contest. This was not an arcane, controlled research study. We could all observe – increasingly – the way such performances were mandatory and coercive in all arms of service industries, including in professional services where I routinely hear examples of junior women accepting 'being hit on' or being belatedly corralled into a client pitch as 'the token female' as part of their apprenticeship. The next time we are served in a restaurant, airplane or office we see how delivery of attractive caring is part of what is being bought. We can understand something of the costs and, at the very least, not succumb to just reinforcing these expectations.

Critiquing bureaucracies and exploring alternatives – Kathy Ferguson

I was a political science scholar before I was a business school one. I had studied many theorists, and critiques, of bureaucracy. But none of them prepared me for the smack in the face that was reading Kathy Ferguson's *The Feminist Case Against Bureaucracy.* Ferguson challenged bureaucratic modes of organizing in a new way, for me anyway. She provided a radical alternative based on feminist theory and the experiences of women.

> The radical feminist hostility to bureaucracy is based on a well-founded, if not yet well-articulated, opposition to the consequences of hierarchical domination for both individuals and the collective. The expanding bureaucratization of the polity carries severe consequences for meaningful participation in public life for women and men.
>
> (Kathy Ferguson, 1984: 83)

Continuing, she warns, 'It is important to remember the complexity of bureaucratic domination, its ability to both *suppress* and *produce* its victims' (italics in original, 1984: 90).

As I've described elsewhere, the emergence of my own feminist consciousness was a slow burn through my undergraduate and immediate postgraduate years. It was ignited through a research project documenting the experiences of women in local government (1984–1987) and then in trying to understand and theorise my experience as a junior woman business school professor (described in Sinclair, 1997; 2000).

The opening chapters of *The Feminist Case* named a real dilemma I was facing: that in the very critiques of gendered arrangements in organizations I was offering, was the possibility that I made traditional systems and structures more robust. Ferguson's prescient warning is that:

> conformity and the abandonment of critical consciousness are the prices of successful performance in the bureaucratic world. An exclusive focus on integrating women into public institutions produces a situation that perpetuates bureaucratic discourse rather than challenging it.
>
> (1984: 29)

The reality check that is *The Feminist Case* refused to allow me to be complacent. Ferguson drew me into an impeccably argued analysis for a continuing radical criticality of dominant wisdom, disciplinary conveniences and shibboleths. Her work ensured I couldn't sink into (or only occasionally) the byways and stale dead ends down which some research of gender and women finds itself. I wrote in the book margin that much of the women-in-management research I was reading at the time was, to use Ferguson's words, 'politically naïve'. It is a view I still hold. Why would men want to willingly give up the power they had worked so hard to acquire?

The Feminist Case Against Bureaucracy is tough reading yet not unhopeful. The final chapter explores in detail a feminist 'alternative to the discursive and institutional practices of bureaucracy in the submerged and devalued experience of women' (ibid: 155). Ferguson maintains this feminist discourse invites a 're-formulation of some of the most central terms of political life: reason, power, community, freedom' (1984: 155), noting that an alternative, non-bureaucratic social order emerges not from writing, but 'as people begin to think and live differently ... pointing to a different set of values, an alternative mode of personal identity and social interaction' (ibid).

A feminist discourse constitutes itself through, Ferguson argues quoting Foucault, 'an insurrection of subjugated knowledges'. It provides critical points of action from which resistance can proceed – and it did for me. The final chapter of *The Feminist Case* is heavily pencilled and asterisked in my copy with connections to two papers I worked on in succession (1992 and 1997). Opposition voices bring power to light and alter that power. I recognised that I could write and teach differently, with feminist principles guiding me.

Ferguson provides arguments for why we should not just study organizations differently but adopt different writing practices, where the reader is invited into participation with the text, not just consumption. She critiques habits of organizational writing, the 'rhetorical implications of which are "unsavoury"' (1994: 89). And she advocates for more and different theory. There are no predictable homilies here thank God! Just a restless determination to see through and past the smokescreens our disciplinary conventions throw up.

For me these arguments were oasis-like because they enabled me to be a critical management scholar (which had felt to me a decidedly blokey and male referential field), as well as a gender scholar. Further, they opened up the possibility of mapping practices of resistance that were most eloquently advocated, and modelled, by women. It was in this context that I began to read and research more widely on sexualities in organizations and how some men's performance of heterosexuality elided naturally with conceptions of leadership. The solution was not the one being advocated in the women's self-help and 'dressing for success' genres. As Rosemary Pringle wrote in *Secretaries Talk*:

> It makes no sense to banish sexuality from the workplace ... It is by making it visible, exposing the masculinity that lurks behind gender-neutrality, asserting women's rights to be subjects rather than objects of sexual discourses, that bureaucracy can be challenged.
>
> (1988: 177)

Ferguson and the wider feminist research I discussed here supported me to move from feeling marginalised, to exercising and owning my power as a scholar. Both Judi Marshall and Kathy Ferguson take women's experiences and their forms of resistance as serious challenges to organizational dogma – in fact, they see the resistances and challenges offered by women and feminist theory as primary grounds for critique.

Impacts of 1980s women writers

Re-reading these three authors' texts and the wider scholarship sitting around them which I savoured – often furtively – through the late 1980s and beyond has pulled up a lot of memories for me. It has filled me with gratitude for this writing. Each identified and spoke organizational phenomena that previous scholars had either missed or devalued as uninteresting or 'deficient' variants on an uninspected male norm. Each was courageous in different ways. Yet there are particular collective legacies of this work that changed organizational and management scholarship, as well as the ambition, intent and style of my own work.

First, they showed that women's experiences of organizations and management were important. The reasons to research women's experiences in organizational studies are moral and political, as well as being a source of change and innovation in traditional structures and norms. Carol Gilligan, pioneer in this endeavour, remarks 'women are more likely to recognize and name the patriarchal story as a false story' (2011). This has also been my experience. Asking women (and using methods which fully hear their experiences) has exposed oppressive racial and gender dynamics that are taken-for-granted and everywhere in organizational life.

Along with other researchers of the period, these authors brought feminist perspectives to propose that organizations could and should be different. In being governed by feminist values and women's knowledges, they offered human-centred views of how organizational life might proceed. Their critical feminist theorising demands we face realities while installing in us not cynicism, but deeper understanding and appetite for change.

Perhaps most wonderfully, from my perspective, they wrote in a more compelling, less pompous and abstracted way compared to many male theorists I had read. In Judi Marshall and Arlie Hochschild's case they invited us, readers, into the world of their research. They shared a sense of why they were on this journey and the movements of their own sense of identity and awakening, through their work. In *Feminist Case Against Bureaucracy*, Kathy Ferguson refused to allow limp excuses in her passion for critique.

Each aimed for and addressed an audience that included but went beyond academics, wanting this wider audience to care about and enact change in the phenomena they explored. *The Managed Heart* succeeded in just this wider way and helped create an audience for in-depth, readable sociology, that Hochschild continued to address in her later books.

As I was sitting down to make final revisions to this chapter, I was also reading some books about women writers of the early modern period, from 1500–1800. My daughter is doing a PhD on one of these writers, Lucrezia Marinella who, among her many poems, essays and books, in 1600 published *The Nobility and Excellence of Women and the Defects and Vices of Men*. The extensive and inventive work of women writers during this period laid the foundations for feminism. They critiqued gendered norms of chastity – to which women's value was tied – problems in gaining power, in speaking, being heard and read. Six centuries later, their contribution is being re-inserted into history, philosophy and accounts of knowledge-creation.

The reason I mention this here is the parallel with this series. Contemporary women scholars face versions of the same pressures as our sixteenth-century counterparts: being ignored, dismissed and ridiculed, having our writing ripped off or its message trivialised. It is our responsibility – not an onerous but a joyful one – to read women's scholarship on management and organizations, to ensure it is appreciated and incorporated in theorising and practice. I recommend you read the original texts – each as relevant to the challenges of today's organizations as when they were written – and later work included in the bibliography below. Read commentaries on their contribution, such as the other chapter in this series on Arlie Hochschild. Notice both the impact on their fields, such as Judi Marshall's pioneering influence on the women and management field, and that their work, such as Ferguson's, deserves to have been much more widely read. While each offers enduring critiques of traditional organizational systems, their gifts are to show alternative ways of being critical scholars, encouraging our resistance, our voices, our creativity and appetites for change.

Recommended reading

Original texts by Judi Marshall, Arlie Hochschild and Kathy Ferguson

Ferguson, K. (1984) *The Feminist Case Against Bureaucracy*. Philadelphia, PA: Temple University Press.

Hochschild, A. (1983) *The Managed Heart: The Commercialization of Human Feelings*. Berkeley, CA: University of California Press.

Marshall, J. (1995) *Women Managers Moving On: Exploring Career and Life Choices*. London: Routledge.

Key academic text

Sinclair, A. (1998) *Doing Leadership Differently: Gender, Power and Sexuality in a Changing Business Culture*. Carlton, VIC: Melbourne University Press.

Accessible resource

Sinclair, A. (2000) Teaching managers about masculinities. *Management Learning* 31(1): 83–101.

References

Baker Miller, J. (1976, 1991 2nd edition) *Toward a New Psychology of Women*. London: Penguin.

Belenky, M., Clinchy, B., Goldberger, N. and Tarule, J. (1986) *Women's Ways of Knowing: The Development of Self, Voice and Mind*. New York, NY: Basic Books.

Bolton, S. (2005) *Emotion Management in the Workplace*. London: Palgrave.

Calás, M. and Smircich, L. (1992) Using the F-word: Feminist theories and the social consequences of organizational research. In: A. Mills and P. Tancred (eds), *Gendering Organizational Analysis*. Newbury Park, CA: Sage Publications, pp. 222–234.

Calás, M. and Smircich, L. (1993) Dangerous Liaisons: The 'feminine-in-management' meets 'globalization'. *Business Horizons* 36(2): 71–81.

Eisenstein, H. (1984) *Contemporary Feminist Thought*. North Sydney, NSW: Allen & Unwin.

Eisenstein, H. (1991) *Gender Shock: Practicing Feminism on Two Continents*. Boston, MA: Beacon Press.

Ferguson, K. (1984) *The Feminist Case Against Bureaucracy*. Philadelphia, PA: Temple University Press.

Ferguson, K. (1994) On bringing more theory, more voices and more politics to the study of organization. *Organization* 1(1): 81–99.

Gilligan, C. (1982) *In a Different Voice*. Boston, MA: Harvard University Press.

Gilligan, C. (2011) Looking back to look forward: Revisiting *In a Different Voice* Classics, Issue 9, 'Defense Mechanisms in Interdisciplinary Approaches to Classical Studies and Beyond'. http://nrs.harvard.edu/urn-3:hul.ebook:CHS_Classicsat.

Grey, C. and Sinclair, A. (2006) Writing differently. *Organization* 13(3): 443–453.

Grieve, N. and Grimshaw, P. (1981) *Australian Women: Feminist Perspectives*. Melbourne, VIC: Oxford University Press.

Hancock, P., Sullivan, K. and Tyler, M. (2015) A touch too much: Negotiating perceptions of masculinity, propriety and proximity in intimate labour. *Organization Studies* 36(12): 1715–1739.

Harding, S. (1987) *Feminism and Methodology*. Bloomington, IN: Indiana University Press.

Hochschild, A. (1983) *The Managed Heart: The Commercialization of Human Feelings*. Berkeley, CA: University of California Press.

Hochschild, A. (1997) *The Time Bind: When Work Becomes Home and Home Becomes Work*. New York, NY: Metropolitan Books.

Hochschild, A. (2016) *Strangers in Their Own Land: Anger and Mourning on the American Right*. New York, NY: The New Press.

hooks, b. (1984) *Feminist Theory from Margin to Centre*. Boston, MA: South End.

Marshall, J. (1984) *Women Managers: Travellers in a Male World*. Chichester: Wiley & Sons.

Marshall, J. (1995) *Women Managers Moving On: Exploring Career and Life Choices*. London: Routledge.

Marshall, J. (2016) *First Person Action Research: Living Life as Inquiry*. London: Sage.

McMurray, R. and Ward, J. (2014) 'Why would you want to do that?': Defining emotional dirty work. *Human Relations* 67(9): 1123–1143.

Pringle, R. (1988) *Secretaries Talk: Sexuality, Power and Work*. Sydney, NSW: Allen & Unwin.

Sinclair, A. (1992) The tyranny of a team ideology. *Organization Studies* 13(4): 611–626.

Sinclair, A. (1994) *Trials at the Top: Chief Executives Talk About Men, Women and the Australian Executive Culture.* Parkville, VIC: The Australian Centre.

Sinclair, A. (1995) Sex and the MBA. *Organization* 2(2): 295–317.

Sinclair, A. (1997) The MBA through women's eyes. *Management Learning* 28(3): 313–330.

Sinclair, A. (1998) *Doing Leadership Differently: Gender, Power and Sexuality in a Changing Business Culture.* Carlton, VIC: Melbourne University Press.

Sinclair, A. (2000) Teaching managers about masculinities. *Management Learning* 31(1): 83–101.

Sinclair, A. (2004) Journey around Leadership. *Discourse: Studies in the Cultural Politics of Education* 25(1): 7–19.

Sinclair, A. (2007) *Leadership for the Disillusioned.* Crows Nest, Australia: Allen & Unwin.

Sinclair, A. (2010) Placing Self: How might we place ourselves differently in studying leadership? *Leadership* 6(4): 447–460.

Sinclair, A. (2011) Being leaders: Identities and identity work in leadership. In: A. Bryman, D. Collinson, K. Grint, B. Jackson and M. Uhl-Bien (eds), *The Sage Handbook of Leadership.* London: Sage, pp 508–517.

Sinclair, A. (2013) Can I really be me? The Challenges for women leaders constructing authenticity. In: D. Ladkin and C. Spiller (eds), *Authentic Leadership: Concepts, Coalescences and Clashes.* Cheltenham, UK: Edward Elgar, pp 239–251.

Sinclair, A. and Ladkin, D. (2018) Writing through the body: Political, personal, practical. In: C. Cassell, A. Cunliffe and G. Grady (eds), *The Sage Handbook of Qualitative Research Methods in Business and Management.* London: Sage, pp 415–428, Ch 25.

Waring, M. (1985) *Women, Politics and Power.* Wellington, NZ: Allen & Unwin.

Waring, M. (1988) *Counting for Nothing.* Wellington, NZ: Allen & Unwin.

5 Luce Irigaray's philosophy of the feminine

Exploring a culture of sexual difference in the study of organizations

Sheena J. Vachhani

Since the publication of *Speculum of the Other Woman*, Luce Irigaray has founded some of what can now be thought of as the central claims of post-structuralist French feminism. Irigaray makes a turn to embodiment where the body is a site for the creative possibilities of the body, and her work initiates visceral and embodied forms of thinking about organizations. Irigaray intervenes in a number of philosophers' work, from Plato to Nietzsche, as a way of unearthing the silent feminine and making it present. Irigaray's work has gained prominence in management and organization studies and this chapter outlines the contribution of her work to ideas around: the question of difference and the ethics of sexual difference; the influence of psychoanalysis and the maternal in her work; critiques around biological essentialism; and, processes and strategies of writing that disturb and disinter conventional textual practices.

Her analysis of Western philosophy centres on the critique of the existence of one subject, the masculine subject conceived through patriarchal order, that is to say the predominance of masculinity for understanding social and symbolic life. In Irigaray's words, 'It is not a matter of toppling that order so as to replace it – that amounts to the same thing in the end – but of disrupting, and modifying it, starting from an "outside" that is exempt, in part, from phallocratic law' (Irigaray, 1985b: 68). Irigaray has been accused of perpetuating essentialist readings of identity and sexed bodies, however, proponents of her work suggest that her writing can be read as a form of strategic or political essentialism (Stone, 2006).

Irigaray was born in Belgium in 1932 and holds doctoral degrees in Philosophy and Linguistics; she also trained as a psychoanalyst. She has also been active in women's movements, especially in France and Italy.

Irigaray's work has predominantly attracted a feminist audience although she is also well positioned as a philosopher, especially in her earlier works. She has been critical of being asked biographical and personal questions. As Whitford (1991a) writes, Irigaray saw this as a distraction or disruption for those engaging with her work based on the well-founded understanding that women are neutralised and reduced through their biography. She was an outspoken critic of psychoanalysis, exemplified in *Speculum of the Other Woman*, first published in 1974, after which she lost her post in the Department of Psychoanalysis at Vincennes (Whitford, 1991a) and was exiled from the École freudienne de Paris founded by Jacques Lacan. As Whitford (1991a) also notes, what is interesting is that her work is a critique from within psychoanalysis. This critique positioned her as an outsider in psychoanalysis and spurred her thinking on a culture of difference driven by social and symbolic change. This chapter continues by developing these threads within Irigaray's oeuvre and discusses how her texts have been used to explore organizational themes such as: sexual difference, psychoanalysis and organizations, and writing materiality in academic practice.

The question of difference in feminist politics: Cultivating a culture of difference

> And what passages are there from the one to the other? You do not come inside me. You follow your own routes through me. But I, am I not a reminder of what you buried in oblivion to build your world? And do you not discover all the past dangers as you return to hollow out this crypt? And, you, are you not a light giving me no light nor life.
>
> (Irigaray, 1992: 36)

Difference has become a central issue in feminist theory (Weedon, 1999; Hekman, 1999; Lennon and Whitford, 1994) and post-structuralism

> has queried the status and explanatory power of general theories (metanarratives) such as liberal humanism and Marxism and produced a discursive shift which – it is often argued – opens up space for alternative voices, new forms of subjectivity, previously marginalised narratives, and new interpretations, meanings and values.
>
> (Weedon, 1999: 4)

As Susan Hekman discusses, differences involve power, 'If we challenge those differences by asserting their opposites, the challenge is necessarily parasitic on the difference itself, not an escape from it' (Hekman, 1999: 11).

Phelan (1999: 56) asserts that discussions concerning identity and difference within feminist politics have centred around

> two lines of cleavage and connection. The first deals with the relations between men and women. Should the goal of feminist politics be for women to assert and achieve sameness with men, or should it be a recognition of women's distinctive, yet valuable, specificity? The second concerns relations amongst women. If we say that "women" are either "the same as" or "different from" men, to which women (and which men) are we referring? It is clear that women differ among themselves as much as men differ from women.

Irigaray attempts to redefine and rearticulate the feminine subject while not reducing the feminine to the same or to one (that is male/masculine).

Irigaray's oeuvre promotes a 'culture of difference' (Irigaray, 1993b). As Fuss (1992) propounds, some critics of Irigaray appear to have missed the figurative character of her *body* language. Irigaray could be said to *re-metaphorise* the female body in a way that reconceptualises the subject as embodied. Irigaray attempts to conjure up an 'other woman', a woman who does not incarnate the patriarchal femininity of Freudian theory.

> The new woman, rather, would be beyond phallocentrism; she would deploy a new, feminine syntax to give symbolic expression to her specificity and difference. Irigaray's most striking attempts to release, conjure up or invent this other woman are lyrical evocations of a non-phallic, feminine sexuality.
>
> (Fraser, 1992: 10)

Essays such as When Our Lips Speak Together (Irigaray, 1985b) evoke an eroticism premised on the continual demonstration of difference through the self-touching of 'two lips'. Neither clitoral nor vaginal, this would be a feminine pleasure that exceeds the binary opposition of activity/passivity, for example (Fraser, 1992). As Irigaray writes,

> My lips are not opposed to generation. They keep the passage open. They accompany birth without holding it to a – closed – place or form. They clasp the whole with their desire. Giving shape, again and again, without stopping. Everything is held together and not held back in their fond embrace. They risk making abyssal anything which would have an origin or roots in one definitive creation.
>
> (Irigaray, 1992: 65–66)

Having outlined the question of difference and the development of a culture of difference, I further this discussion by exploring the influence of psychoanalysis in Irigaray's work.

Irigaray, psychoanalysis and studies of work and organization

Irigaray's work has gained prominence in organization studies in recent years and attention has tended to focus on the organization of sexual difference brought out in her work, rather than on its psychoanalytical tenets (notable exceptions being Fotaki, 2009a; Kenny & Bell, 2011; Metcalfe, 2005; Vachhani, 2012). For example, Oseen (1997) explores the symbolization of sexual difference in relation to leadership while Atkin, Hassard and Wolfram Cox (2007; see also Hassard, Keleman & Wolfram Cox, 2008) use the concepts of residue and excess at the heart of Irigaray's mimetic strategy, a key feature of her writing explored later in this chapter, to push taken-for-granted discourses to their limit. Vachhani (2015) discusses the transformative and activist potential of feminine writing that offers a practical politics for changing organizations. Metcalfe (2005) casts a critical eye on the exploration of Irigaray's work in critical management studies, especially how sameness and difference are reinforced by phallocentric discourses (that is to say, thinking that centres around the presence or absence of the phallus). In contrast, Fotaki (2009) provides a close examination of Irigaray's feminist psychoanalytic approach in relation to academic work. Vachhani (2012) also draws on the psychoanalytical tenets of Irigaray's work to address the political and ethical dilemmas that arise from the subordination of the feminine. Building on these discussions, Fotaki et al. (2014) call for a feminist écriture of/for organization studies that does not suppress nor conceal possibilities for understanding difference as a recognition of the feminine.

Irigaray's concerns are with the imaginary and symbolic, and in developing an account of subjectivity that acknowledges the existence of different sexes, bodies, forms of desire and ways of knowing (Grosz, 1990). The value and importance of her theoretical engagement with the maternal-feminine provide resources for critically evaluating psychoanalysis as it has been developed in organization studies. In Irigaray's terms, the systematic suppression of femininity, thus the suppression of difference, has reduced women to the 'economy of the same' (see Whitford, 1991a, 1991b; Irigaray, 2000).

The exclusion of the maternal from the history of Western philoso-phy, and indeed culture, represents for Irigaray (1992, 1993a, 1999, for example), the banishment of women. Irigaray addresses the politi-cal and ethical dilemmas arising from this position, significant for better understanding gendered relations in organizations, developing a femi-nine imaginary and new spaces of symbolization and representation for women. Irigaray's search for a female imaginary is perhaps why some critics have labelled her work utopian (Fuss, 1992; Stone, 2003). To sum up Irigaray's position:

> We can assume that any theory of the subject has always been appropri-ated by the "masculine". When she submits to [such a] theory, woman fails to realize that she is renouncing the specificity of her own rela-tionship to the imaginary. Subjecting herself to objectivization in dis-course – by being "female". Re-objectivizing her own self whenever she claims to identify herself "as" a masculine subject. A "subject" that would re-search itself as lost (maternal-feminine) "object"?
>
> (Irigaray, 1985a: 133)

Irigaray argues for 'a self-defined woman who would not be satisfied with sameness, but whose otherness and difference would be given social and symbolic representation' (Whitford, 1991b: 24–25). Of Irigaray's relation-ship with psychoanalysis, Grosz writes,

> Irigaray's early works must be positioned in the context of her reading and critique of Freudian/Lacanian psychoanalytic theory. Her rela-tion to it remains extremely significant in all of her works, whether or not they specifically address psychoanalytic terms and concepts, providing a paradigm of the ways in which her position is always ambiguous, always tenuously internal to the discipline or theory she challenges. At the same time, these works position themselves at those points outside of the founding terms of theories or knowledges in those places, intolerable to and expelled by them – their vulnerable underbelly.
>
> (Grosz, 1994: 336)

Irigaray's (1985a) tactic is for a close reading in which she separates the text into fragments, weaving between Freud's words and her own. 'She never sums up the meaning of Freud's text, nor binds all her commen-taries, questions, associations into a unified representation, a coherent interpretation. Her commentaries are full of loose ends and unanswered questions' (Gallop, 1982: 56; Fielding, 2003; Irigaray, 1991b). Irigaray is significantly influenced by the explanatory power of psychoanalysis in relation to the construction and reproduction of patriarchal forms of subjectivity by situating Freud, for example, as a symptom of a particular social or cultural economy (Grosz, 1990) and psychoanalysis as symptomatic of an underlying phallocentric structure that governs dominant ideas around gender.

Irigaray is positioned distinctively in the text, and this forms an important aspect of understanding her approach to reading Freud and Lacan. For Irigaray, a Lacanian theory of the subject is only representative of a masculine account of subject formation and social life. As Grosz argues of Lacan,

> If "style" is the object of psychoanalytic teaching and training, then Lacan's style is deliberately provocative, stretching terms to the limits of their coherence, creating a text that is difficult to enter and ultimately impossible to master. His "style" contains the same evasions, the same duplicit speech as the unconscious itself.
>
> (Grosz, 1990: 17)

Irigaray, while taking Lacan's understanding of metaphor and metonymy seriously, also chooses to read him according to his own proclamations, that is to say, literally (Grosz, 1990).

Strategic essentialism

In response to criticisms of biological essentialism, it is often argued that Irigaray engages in what has been termed 'strategic essentialism' (Burke et al., 1994; Grosz, 1989; Stone, 2006; Whitford, 1994). Significantly, Stone (2006) explores the idea of strategic essentialism as a way to negotiate the divide between unity and difference in feminist projects as critiques of patriarchy. Strategic essentialism (a term attributed to Gayatri Chakravorty Spivak according to Stone, 2006) seeks to confront the notion that:

> If women share no common characteristics, they cannot readily be expected to mobilise in response to a common plight, or around any shared political identity or sense of allegiance. Confronted by this problem, several theorists began to advocate a new, "strategic", form of essentialism. According to this, we should acknowledge that essentialism is false: women have no shared location or unitary female biology. Nonetheless, we should continue to act, strategically, as if essentialism were true, where this furthers political purposes.
>
> (Stone, 2006: 29)

Essentialist preconceptions, as Stone further explains, are deeply embedded in dominant symbolic structures, so much so that they can be overcome only when confronted and, paradoxically, repeated and redoubled. She writes:

> crucially this form of strategic essentialism is *non-realist*. It does not hold that women really have essential characteristics independently of cultural practices but, rather, claims that many traditions and practices (falsely) insist that women have such characteristics, traditions which can be challenged only through the strategic affirmation of precisely those essential characteristics on which they insist.
>
> (Stone, 2006: 29)

The emergence of the concept of strategic essentialism suggested to those reading Irigaray in the late 1980s and early 1990s that her detractors had relied on a rather oversimplified view of essentialism and its political potential. 'There could, it had emerged, be different "kinds of essentialisms", with varying political consequences' (Stone, 2006: 29) which could, inter alia, be politically transformative. Whitford (1994: 16) echoes this point by saying

> the binary pair essentialism/antiessentialism has been put into question. This enables essentialism to be interpreted as a *position* rather than as an ontology, and Irigaray to be interpreted as a strategist … rather than as an obscurantist prophet of essential biological or psychic difference.

Stone (2006: 30) also succinctly notes that Irigaray 'does not intend her essentialism to describe the female body realistically but to reaffirm traditional representations of the female (through sustained mimicry and paraphrase of philosophical texts) in a way which operates, politically, to subvert their meaning'. It is adopted in a temporary and deliberate manner, based not on biological differences but language where woman is not represented (Grosz, 1994; Whitford, 1991b). Having explored the question of feminine difference, psychoanalysis and strategic essentialism in Irigaray's work, the chapter now turns to exploring her use of mimesis, especially in her earlier philosophical texts.

Irigaray's style

Mimicry and philosophical texts

Since the introduction of *Speculum of the Other Woman*[1], Irigaray has founded some of what could now be seen as the central claims of French feminism. She has been labelled a 'gynocentric' (Young, 1985, cited in Fraser and Bartky, 1992) critic often seen as having essentialist readings of identity (cf. Deutscher, 1997; Fuss, 1992), as discussed above. Whitford (1991b) and Grosz (1994) among others have argued that she draws on language to assert how woman is not represented and deploys a style that suffuses poetry with logic and hovers between politics and love, philosophy and psychoanalysis (Martin, 2003). This approach enacts a kind of mimicry and is a challenge to philosophy and to psychoanalysis, in which Irigaray aims to speak to Freud, Plato, Heidegger and Nietzsche, to name a handful, which elicits dialogue while speaking passionately, poetically and politically. The textual strategy of mimicry prevalent in the early and middle stages of her work ensued from her analysis of the Western tradition as one that could not bear the representation of a feminine subject, or the subject as feminine. With the laws of discourse and the symbolic order constructed on masculine terms, her question was: How could she speak without assuming the masculine genre? (Martin, 2003). Irigaray (1985a: 140) writes,

> He must challenge her for power, for productivity. He must resurface the earth with this floor of the ideal. Identify with the law-giving father, with his proper names, his desires for making capital, in every sense of the word, desires that prefer the possession of territory, which includes language, to the exercise of his pleasures, with the exception of his pleasure in trading women – fetishized objects, merchandise of whose value he stands surety – with his peers.

Irigaray, however, has not engaged in such a style lightly (Martin, 2003) and has always been cautious about the efficacy of writing differently to bring about change (cf. Irigaray, 1993b).

An Ethics of Sexual Difference (1993)[2] and *This Sex Which is Not One* (1985b), along with *Speculum of the Other Woman* (1985a), are arguably Irigaray's most influential texts, existing alongside her compelling 'elemental works' such as *Marine Lover of Friedrich Nietzsche* (1991), *The Forgetting of Air in Martin Heidegger* (1999) and *Elemental Passions* (1999). Through a strategy of mimicry, Irigaray pushes psychoanalytic discourses (among more traditionally philosophical discourses) to their limits, thus showing their deficiency and poverty in subordinating femininity and ultimately leaving it unrepresented. The dialogue, for example, that Irigaray provides with Heidegger in *The Forgetting of Air in Martin Heidegger* echoes, illustrates and reflects her style, and echoes a fundamental difference in writing.

> There is always difference. If one listens to her words, one hears a dialogue, a going back and forth meant to take the path of his thinking

further; she enacts the to and fro motion of criss-crossing, a folding-over relation, that asserts a limit between the two voices even as there are penetrations and mixings.

(Fielding, 2003: 2)

She adopts 'a double style', a style of amorous relations, writing in a move toward '[t]he wedding between the body and language' (Irigaray, 2000: 17 also cited in Fielding, 2003). By way of illustrating this theme, in *To Be Two* Irigaray outlines how to read *The Forgetting of Air* in which she cares about the gaps – the places where she feels Heidegger in this instance has not pushed his thinking far enough (due to a neglect of sexual difference). She takes Heideggerian terms and uses them in a way that mimics, yet continues and highlights the lacunae in his argument, as if inhabiting Heidegger's line of thought. Irigaray opens up a discussion with Heidegger in this way, moving through his arguments, questioning, sealing, unpicking and re-stitching his thought. Irigaray thus mimics but also invents dialogue almost as 'lovers' quarrels', to move through Heidegger's words, to fold over them but not to write over them, to give and take in one movement. The structure of books such as *Speculum of the Other Woman* also forms part of her attempts to jam the theoretical machinery and present challenges for embodied writing. Irigaray propounds,

> Strictly speaking, *Speculum* has no beginning or end. The architectonics of the text, or texts, confounds the linearity of an outline, the teleology of discourse, within which there is no possible place for the "feminine," except the traditional place of the repressed, the censured.
>
> (Irigaray, 1985b: 68)

Dialogue and embodied writing

The constructed dialogue with her interlocutors provides a closeness and intimate philosophical readings. Irigaray's text communicates but simultaneously always leaves breathing room for the reader, for an other to come. As Whitford notes, many of her philosophical texts 'ventriloquise', they speak with others' words but they are also made her own: 'Whether one recognises the courses or not depends on one's familiarity with the philosopher, since inverted commas are seldom used' (Whitford, 1991a: 9). The blurring of boundaries within her texts makes Irigaray's style dense and mellifluous. However, the structured pauses sometimes risk becoming obscurantist when lost in translation: the texts often evoke no answering echo. The textual scholarship needed to undertake Irigaray's texts make them elusive, dazzling, deliberately polysemic and difficult to unravel (Whitford, 1991a: 9).

The intimate tussles with philosophers and the miming of dialogue (Irigaray, 1985a; 1985b; 1991; 1999) both offer critical possibilities for invoking the feminine. The imaginary or not yet realised feminine subjectivity Irigaray writes is formulated in a way that offers possibilities for change, of women in dialogue finding their own locution that also weaves hopes for the future through her texts. As Irigaray writes:

> Later comes the task, the work. Heavy, but light. Of different resonances, its breath fills the air, making a bridge between heaven and earth. Its ranges balance the profundity of silence, the absolute of solitude. The notes and tones vary unless they return to the single breath. The body becomes a musician, if it does not remain solely at the breath. In order to be incarnated, to arrive at your incarnation, it changes tones, methods. It feels, looks, listens, sings or speaks: to you, to her. Energy is made sense, inclination is made sensibility, desire becomes interiority.
>
> (Irigaray, 2000: 61)

Here, Irigaray writes the body attending to its senses, and as with the touching of two lips, silence becomes a way of communicating, a way which cannot be interrupted by phallocentric discourse but is *felt* or experienced *between* women rather than *for* women. By attending to tone, breath and silence she is *creating* this difference: writing the sensory and sensible. This keeps her project vital and visionary although some have felt uneasy with the utopian elements in her texts where the past, present and future are interwoven throughout.

It is the creative power of imagination that one can celebrate in Irigaray's work and as Whitford (1991b) argues, one cannot fix her in a single meaning or a single moment of text. The most productive readings of her texts are dynamic and engage and exchange with her work as an interlocutor, as she produces writing that cannot be reduced to a narrative or a commentary. Burke et al.'s (1994a) edited collection demonstrates such an engagement. Braidotti's contribution, for example, examines ways in which Irigaray's oeuvre provides a 'systematic and multifaceted attempt to redesign our understanding of the thinking subject, in a language and a form of representation that adequately renders women's experience' (Braidotti, 1994: 111), in which Irigaray sexualises, through the feminine, the very structures of subjectivity. By examining the becoming-woman, Braidotti shows that the process of becoming is primarily a process of repetition, of mimesis, of cyclical returns.

Irigaray also evokes an embodied dialogue in the section *Speaking of Immemorial Waters* in *Marine Lover of Friedrich Nietzsche*, where she writes, 'How should I love you if to speak to you were possible. And yet I still love you too well in my silence to remember the movement of my own becoming. Perpetually am I troubled, stirred, frozen, or smothered by the noise of your death' (Irigaray, 1991: 3). By engaging in a double-style of mimicry and dialogue Irigaray forces the interlocutor/reader into play in order to read her enigmatic texts where the response is not a passive consumption but a productive process.

Furthermore, Hodge (1994: 194) in her essay Irigaray Reading Heidegger articulates this difference and how Irigaray reads back into philosophical and heroic texts a subversive femininity that is both contained and expelled. For example, as she notes in *Speculum of the Other Woman*, 'She does not look for an alternative tradition of forgotten or undervalued texts, written by women. She looks for the silencing gesture of these alternative voices in the heroic texts themselves, and seeks by brushing these texts against the grain *to empower that silenced energy.*'

This is most apparent in Irigaray's re-writing of the philosophers (cf. Chanter, 1995), where she demonstrates how the death and transfiguration of Socrates inscribed at the beginning of philosophy conceals the death of the mother. Irigaray empowers the silenced energy of the texts in her re-writing of the myth of the cave in the section Plato's Hystera of *Speculum*:

> "While carrying their burdens, some of them, as you would expect, are talking, others silent." As you would expect. Really and truly? Yes, you would expect it, given the systems of duplication, the rules of duplicity, that organize the cave. For if everyone talked, and talked at once, the background noise would make it difficult or even impossible for the doubling process known as an echo to occur. The reflection of sound would be *spoiled* if different speakers uttered different things at the same time. Sounds would thereby become ill defined, fuzzy, inchoate, indistinct, devoid of figures that can be reflected and reproduced. If everyone spoke, and spoke at once, the silence of the others would no longer form the *background* necessary to highlight or outline the words of some, or of one. Silence or blanks function here in two ways to allow replication. *Of likeness*.
>
> (Irigaray, 1985a: 256–257)

In this excerpt, Irigaray draws on the lack of voice for women by rewriting Plato's myth. Irigaray rewrites the myth by taking Plato's words and introducing another way of reading them, in this instance by re-reading sound. She pushes his ideas to their limit through mimicry and creating a dialogue. She uses the interiority of his thought and writes with the body in order to re-organize the cave. This close reading serves to show how Irigaray portrays language as suppressive to the needs of women and makes a turn to embodiment where the body is a site for the creative possibilities of the sexually specific body through focusing on the visceral and embodied.

Implications for understanding gendered relations in organizations

For organizations, replete with relationships of domination and subordination, Irigaray provides a theoretical perspective that examines who has claims to knowledge or legitimate voice, and the social/discursive relations which sustain these intersections. This, in turn, exposes 'the importance of the structure masculinity/femininity in sustaining the durability of practices, discourses, and forms of signification that allow certain activities the claim of knowledge, while disallowing others' (Calás and Smircich, 1991: 571; Martin, 1990). It is to these critical possibilities that we should look in order to change the organizations in which we work. Without such modes of ethical being we are destined to be 'the same ... Same ... Always the same' (Irigaray, 1985b: 205).

Höpfl (2011: 28) notes, Irigaray

> is identifying the problem of what it is to be a woman within the phallogocentric discourse: what it is to be constructed in a way which conforms to patriarchal notions of order and authority, and what it is to be regulated by representations which are at variance with embodied experience.

Many have argued that Irigaray's focus on love between women is a way of realising a feminine language that breaks patriarchal language structures through the insistence on sexually specific subjects rather than the mediation of one by the other (what she refers to as 'the other of the same', that is the self-same relations of phallogocentrism, or how language is structured in a way that only represents the masculine subject, see Vachhani, 2019).

As Irigaray writes,

> If we keep speaking sameness, if we speak to each other as men have been doing for centuries, as we have been taught to speak, we'll miss each other, fail ourselves. Again ... Words will pass through our bodies, above our heads. They'll vanish and we'll be lost. Far off, up high. Absent from ourselves: we'll be spoken machines, speaking machines. Enveloped in proper skins, but our own. Withdrawn into proper names, violated by them. Not yours, not mine. We don't have any. We change names as men exchange us, exchanged by them, to be so changeable.
>
> (Irigaray, 1985b: 205)

This thinking offers us new ways of understanding discrimination in the workplace, by providing a way of re-imagining femininity such that we can open up new spaces of symbolization and representation for women (Vachhani, 2019).

As examined earlier, Irigaray explores identity which is assumed in language within a particular (patriarchal) symbolic system in which the only possible subject-position is masculine. Within this system, the only feminine identity available to women is that of 'defective' or 'castrated' men; women are not symbolically self-defined (Whitford, 1991b: 3). This approach helps understand women's role in leadership in a more expansive and theoretically rich manner beyond representations of women leaders as overly masculine, bossy or aggressive (Pullen and Vachhani, 2017).

The concepts of proximity and amorous exchange are central in Irigaray's texts which constitute a rethinking of ethics, as embodied ethics. As Whitford (1991b: 165) writes,

> the amorous exchange is not the exchange of commodities but a mode of ethical being. The horizon opened up by the woman's accession to her own space-time is that of fertility and creation … In order to become a woman, it seems, it is first necessary to rethink all the categories which structure our thought and experience. It is not just a question of inventing some new terms, but of a total symbolic redistribution.

Creating fairer organizations demands consideration of gendered difference or, as Irigaray writes, an ethics of sexual difference: 'that is, an ethics which recognizes the subjectivity of each sex, would have to address the symbolic division which allocates the material, corporeal, sensible, 'natural' to the feminine, and the spiritual, ideal, intelligible, transcendental to the masculine' (Whitford, 1991b: 149).

To end, as Toye (2010: 47) notes, 'Irigaray constantly emphasizes the space of mediation between two subjects, what figures are used in our culture to convey this space, and how, by offering alternative figures to occupy this space, might a revolution in thought and ethics occur'. Such a culture of difference succeeds traditional, dualistic thinking as the hierarchical relationship between masculine and feminine in organizations. What we learn from Irigaray, and also Höpfl's foundational work in the field of work and organization, are the ways in which mastery and rationality have disciplining effects. Feminine writing and ethical difference, through Irigaray, inhabit a political position, one that insinuates resistance (Höpfl, 2011) and which identifies organizations as sites that are not able to bear the weight of the feminine and insists on the self-definition of women in the workplace.

Notes

1 Originally published in French in 1974.
2 Dates shown denote the first translated imprint in Great Britain.

Recommended reading

Original text by Luce Irigaray

Irigaray, L (1993) *An Ethics of Sexual Difference*. Trans. C. Burke and G.C. Gill. London: Athlone.

Key academic text

Vachhani, S.J. (2012) The Subordination of the Feminine? Developing a Critical Feminist Approach to the Psychoanalysis of Organizations. *Organization Studies*, 33(9): 1237–1255.

Accessible resource

Jones, R. (2011) *Irigaray*. Cambridge: Polity Press.
Whitford, M. (1991) *Luce Irigaray – Philosophy in the Feminine*. London: Routledge.

References

Atkin, I., Hassard, J., and Wolfram Cox, J. (2007) Excess and Mimesis in Organization Theory: Emancipation from Within? *Culture and Organization*, 13(2): 145–156.
Braidotti, R. (1994) Of Bugs and Women: Irigaray and Deleuze on the Becoming-Woman. In: C. Burke, N. Schor and M. Whitford (Eds) *Engaging with Irigaray*. New York: Columbia University Press.
Burke, C., Schor, N. and Whitford, M. (Eds) (1994) *Engaging with Irigaray – Feminist Philosophy and Modern European Thought*. Columbia: Columbia University Press.
Calás, M.B. and Smircich, L. (1991) Voicing Seduction to Silence Leadership. *Organization Studies*, 12(4): 567–602.
Chanter, T. (1995) *Ethics of Eros – Irigaray's Rewriting of the Philosophers*. London: Routledge.
Deutscher, P. (1997) *Yielding Gender: Feminism, Deconstruction and the History of Philosophy*. London: Routledge.
Fielding, H. (2003) Questioning Nature: Irigaray, Heidegger and the Potentiality of Matter. *Continental Philosophy Review*, 36(1): 1–26.

Fotaki, M. (2009) The Unwanted Body of Man or Why is it so Difficult for Women to Make it in Academe? A Feminist Psychoanalytic Approach. In: M. Özbilgin (Ed.) *Equality, Diversity and Inclusion at Work: A Research Companion*. Cheltenham, UK: Edward Elgar (pp. 57–71).

Fotaki, M., Metcalfe, B. and Harding, N. (2014) Writing Materiality into Management and Organization Studies Through and with Luce Irigaray. *Human Relations*, 67(10): 1239–1263.

Fraser, N. (1992) The Uses and Abuses of French Discourse Theories for Feminist Politics. In: N. Fraser and S.L. Bartky (Eds) *Revaluing French Feminism – Critical Essays on Difference, Agency and Culture*. Bloomington: Indiana University Press.

Fraser, N. and Bartky, S.L. (Eds) (1992) *Revaluing French Feminism – Critical Essays on Difference, Agency and Culture*. Bloomington: Indiana University Press.

Fuss, D.J. (1992) Essentially Speaking: Luce Irigaray's Language of Essence. In: N. Fraser and S.L. Bartky (Eds) *Revaluing French Feminism – Critical Essays on Difference, Agency and Culture*. Bloomington: Indiana University Press.

Gallop, J. (1982) *Feminism and Psychoanalysis: The Daughter's Seduction*. London: Macmillan.

Grosz, E. (1989) *Sexual Subversions: Three French Feminists*. Sydney: Allen & Unwin.

Grosz, E. (1990) *Jacques Lacan: A Feminist Introduction*. London: Routledge.

Grosz, E. (1994) The Hetero and the Homo: The Sexual Ethics of Luce Irigaray. In: C. Burke, N. Schor and M. Whitford (Eds) *Engaging with Irigaray*. New York: Columbia University Press (pp. 335–350).

Hassard, J., Keleman, M. and Wolfram Cox, J. (2008) *Disorganization Theory: Explorations in Alternative Organizational Analysis*. London: Routledge.

Hekman, S. (1999) Identity Crises: Identity, Identity Politics and Beyond. In: S. Hekman (Ed,) *Feminism, Identity and Difference*. Essex: Frank Cass.

Hodge, J. (1994) Irigaray Reading Heidegger. In: C. Burke, N. Schor and M. Whitford (Eds) *Engaging with Irigaray*. New York: Columbia University Press.

Höpfl, H. (2011) Women's writing. In: E.L. Jeanes, D. Knights and P. Yancey Martin (Eds) *Handbook of Gender, Work and Organization*. Chichester: John Wiley & Sons (pp. 25–36).

Irigaray, L. (1985a) *Speculum of the Other Woman*. Trans. G.C. Gill. New York: Cornell University Press.

Irigaray, L. (1985b) *This Sex Which is Not One*. Trans. C. Porter. New York: Cornell University Press.

Irigaray, L. (1991) *Marine Lover of Friedrich Nietzsche*. Trans. G.C. Gill. New York: Columbia University Press.

Irigaray, L. (1992) *Elemental Passions*. Trans. J. Collie and J. Still. London: Athlone.

Irigaray, L. (1993a) *Sexes and Genealogies*. Trans. G.C. Gill. New York: Columbia University Press.

Irigaray, L. (1993b) *Je, Tu, Nous – Toward a Culture of Difference*. Trans. A. Martin. London: Routledge.

Irigaray, L. (1999) *The Forgetting of Air in Martin Heidegger*. Trans. M.B. Mader. Austin, TX: University of Texas Press.

Irigaray, L. (2000) *To Be Two*. Trans. M.M. Rhodes and M.F. Cocito-Monoc. London: Athlone.

Kenny, K. and Bell, E. (2011) Representing the Successful Managerial Body. In: E. Jeanes, D. Knights and P. Yancey Martin (Eds) *Handbook of Gender, Work and Organization*. Oxford: Wiley-Blackwell (pp. 163–176).

Lennon, K. and Whitford, M. (Eds) (1994) *Knowing the Difference – Feminist Perspectives in Epistemology*. London: Routledge.

Martin, A. (2003) Introduction – Luce Irigaray and the Culture of Difference. *Theory, Culture and Society*, 20(3): 1–12.

Martin, J. (1990) Deconstructing Organizational Taboos: The Suppression of Gender Conflict in Organizations. *Organization Science*, 1(4): 339–359.

Metcalfe, B. (2005) Exiling the Feminine? Re-Imagining Luce Irigaray in the Philosophy of Organization. *Paper presented at the Critical Management Studies Conference*. 4–6 July 2005, Judge Institute of Management, University of Cambridge, Cambridge, UK.

Oseen, C. (1997) Luce Irigaray, Sexual Difference and Theorizing Leaders and Leadership. *Gender, Work and Organization*, 4(3): 170–184.

Phelan, S. (1999) Bodies, Passions and Citizenship. In: S. Hekman (Ed.) *Feminism, Identity and Difference*. Essex: Frank Cass.

Pullen, A. and Vachhani, S.J. (2017) A Leadership Ethics of Sexual Difference? In: A. Bolsø, S.O. Sørensen and S.H.B. Svendsen (Eds) *Bodies, Symbols and Organizational Practice: The Gendered Dynamics of Power*. London/New York: Routledge.

Stone, A. (2006) *Luce Irigaray and the Philosophy of Sexual Difference*. New York: Cambridge University Press.

Stone, A. (2003) The Sex of Nature: A Reinterpretation of Irigaray's Metaphysics and Political Thought. *Hypatia*, 18(3): 60–84.

Toye, M.E. (2010) Towards a Poethics of Love: Poststructuralist Feminist Ethics and Literary Creation. *Feminist Theory*, 11(1): 39–55.

Vachhani, S.J. (2012) The Subordination of the Feminine? Developing a Critical Feminist Approach to the Psychoanalysis of Organizations. *Organization Studies*, 33(9): 1237–1255.

Vachhani, S.J. (2015) Organizing Love — Thoughts on the Transformative and Activist Potential of Feminine Writing. *Gender, Work and Organization*, 22(2): 148–162.

Vachhani, S.J. (2019) Rethinking the Politics of Writing Differently Through *Écriture Féminine*. *Management Learning*, 50(1): 11–23.

Weedon, C. (1999) *Feminism, Theory and the Politics of Difference*. Oxford: Blackwell.

Whitford, M. (1991a) Introductory Chapters. In: L. Irigaray (Ed.) *The Irigaray Reader*. Oxford: Blackwell.

Whitford, M. (1991b) *Luce Irigaray – Philosophy in the Feminine*. London: Routledge.

Whitford, M. (1994) Reading Irigaray in the Nineties. In: C. Burke, N. Schor and M. Whitford (Eds) *Engaging with Irigaray*. New York: Columbia University Press.
Young, I. (1985) Humanism, Gynocentrism and Feminist Politics. *Hypatia*, 8(3): 173–183.

6 Situating knowledges through feminist objectivity in organization studies

Donna Haraway and the Partial Perspective

Ajnesh Prasad, Paulina Segarra and Cristian E. Villanueva

While the early years of the second-wave feminist movement were pre-occupied with addressing the interests of white, middle- and upper-class heterosexual women, the 1980s was an epoch that was punctuated by an invigorated form of representational politics for feminist theorizing and feminist practice. Among the voices that were interjected into the feminist movement of the period were those 'representing' *third-world feminism*—a (perhaps overly) broad label invested in rendering intelligible the experiences of heterogeneous women across those geographies constituted as the Global South. Third-world feminism, when read as an offshoot of the second-wave feminist movement, gained prominence mainly through the publication of texts by two notable scholars who were born and raised in India, but attended graduate school in the United States: Chandra Talpade Mohanty and Gayatri Chakrovorty Spivak.

Mohanty (1984) offered an incisive critique into how white feminist writers of Western origin engaged in a project of ethnocentricism, intentionally or otherwise, through the imprudent deployment of non-Western or *other* woman as a static analytical category. The ethnocentricism to be found in the works of these white feminist writers engendered, among other detrimental outcomes, the homogenization of the varied and the widely diverse experiences of non-Western women and, concomitantly, the negation of the salient differences between constituents of this group. Spivak (1988) extended this line of critique further by illuminating the problematic discourse that emerges as a corollary of the colonial interventions into certain cultural practices that were inscribed onto the bodies of colonized women. Focusing her empirical gaze on the practice of *sati* in India—widow self-immolation—Spivak demonstrates how such an intervention constructed the ideological, and the now well recited, discourse of 'white men saving brown women from brown men' (p. 297).

The interrelated set of critiques leveled by Mohanty and Spivak demanded greater reflexivity among feminists so as to avoid the tacit ethnocentricism that undergirded the early foundation of the second-wave feminist movement. Specifically, feminist thinkers were asked to be mindful of not making claims that might reinscribe ethnocentricism and, by extension, south/north power hierarchies. A logical outcome of the trend towards greater reflexivity was a quandary for feminist scholars pertaining to the question, *who can speak for whom?* This question is distilled from a broader consideration on whether feminist academics (or any other conscientious scholar for that matter) possessed the legitimate authority to engage in debates about 'other' women's social, political, and economic disenfranchisement without reifying the paternalistic discourse that Mohanty and Spivak decried some three decades ago. A non-affirmative response to this question would justify the position of cultural relativism; which would, in effect, disallow feminists situated in the West to intervene in debates that mainly affect the material conditions of non-Western women's lives. These debates would include, for instance, those over female genital mutilation, female infanticide, widow sacrifice, and acid violence. This ultimately raises the question: How can feminists who are geographically positioned in Western spaces engage in discourses that relate to *other* women without reifying the discursive logic of ethnocentricism?

Donna Haraway, a feminist theorist who wrote during the same period as Mohanty and Spivak, proffers an answer to this question. Unlike many other Western-based feminist writers of the day, Haraway was mindful of feminist theory's tendency to problematically construct 'the essentialized Third World Woman,' and she foresaw the resultant dangers in invoking such an analytical category (Haraway, 1988, p. 586). At the same time, Haraway was equally suspicious of silencing the various material conditions that affect the lives of marginalized women at different geographical sites by relegating it to the purview of cultural relativism. In intricately balancing both of these cautionary thoughts, Haraway provides a set of theoretical insights that, first, disavows the ethnocentricism underlying universal truth-claims and, second, allows feminists to responsibly engage in discourses about 'other' women in an effort to catalyze social change. Namely, her ideas of feminist objectivity, the partial perspective, and situated knowledges, impugn Western ethnocentricism though they, concurrently, render permissive a certain axiological discourse about culturally embedded practices.

Before proceeding, a caveat pertaining to our use of the term '*other*' woman merits note. By this term, we bridge two ideas. Adopting the classic meaning of 'fundamental Otherness,' we refer to that woman who comes from cultures that are fabricated as being ontologically different than the West (read: non-west) (Spiro, 1986, p. 262). However, we also layer post-colonial considerations into the meaning by mobilizing the term to describe the woman who is rendered exotic by being assumed to be from less progressive locations than the West (Abu-Lughod, 2002; Said, 1978). Thus, the '*other*' woman represents an essentialized category, socially constructed with the specific dual intent of: i) contributing to the symbiotic and co-dependent production of the equally essentialized identity of the liberated Western woman, and, ii) reifying south/north, east/west power relations (see Abu-Lughod, 2002).

The remainder of this chapter is presented in four sections. First, we provide a brief biographical sketch of Haraway. Second, we outline the debate over universalism versus relativism by identifying some of the main principles of each position. Third, we present a targeted review of Haraway's article that is the subject of this chapter, by focusing specifically on her concepts of feminist objectivity, situated knowledges, and the partial perspective. Fourth, we examine how a few critical scholars in organization and management studies have engaged with 'other' women's experiences. In this section, we also explain how such efforts will only be further catalyzed by Haraway's ideas insofar as they present a deconstructive intervention into this debate over universalism versus relativism. Fifth, we close the chapter with some concluding remarks.

Donna Haraway: a biographical sketch

Born in 1944, Donna Haraway earned her undergraduate degree from Colorado College, for which she majored in zoology and completed dual minors in philosophy and English. In 1972, she earned her PhD in biology from Yale University. During the course of her doctorate, she also gained further exposure to philosophy as well as the history of science and medicine. The intersection between the natural sciences and the humanities that marked her education would come to inform much of her research throughout her scholarly career. Haraway held academic appointments at the University of Hawaii and John Hopkins University, before assuming a post in the prominent History of Consciousness program at the University of California at Santa Cruz in 1980, from where today she has retired with the title of Distinguished Professor Emerita.

Haraway first received critical acclaim for scholarly work following the publication of her 1985 essay, 'A manifesto for cyborgs: Science, technology, and socialist feminism in the 1980s.' As one of the authors of this chapter has described elsewhere:

> This essay, almost immediately, became a watershed text for feminist theory and for, what was at the time, the inchoate field of feminist science studies. Interweaving ideas that were playful and imaginative with an incisive critique of the totalizing essentialism that was the ironic hallmark of the myriad strands of the second-wave feminist movement—encompassing, but not limited to, Marxist, psychoanalytic and radical feminist approaches—Haraway conscientiously articulates the politics of a monstrous creature of the post-gender world: the cyborg.
>
> (Prasad, 2016a, p. 432)

For its deft talent in disarticulating the essentialist and the bifurcated boundaries between culture and nature—and the other socially constructed dichotomies that emerge thereof—this essay positioned Haraway as a mainstay within feminist scholarship. It would be her subsequent article, 'Situated knowledges: The science question in feminism and the privilege of partial perspective' (1988), however, that would anoint her as being among the most influential feminist theorists to date. We will discuss this trailblazing article after briefly outlining the polemical debate over universalism versus relativism, to which her article is especially germane.

Universalism versus relativism

Before outlining Haraway's argument, we first lay out the underlying debate in which she intervenes: that is, universalism versus relativism. This debate has preoccupied much attention in several social science disciplines—though it holds, obviously, a ubiquitous space in anthropology—and has become bifurcated to such an extent that holding aspects of each position is largely considered to be philosophically incommensurable. Namely, with few exceptions (e.g., Dembour, 2001), universalism and relativism are read to be ontologically antithetical to one another with no tenable path available by which to mediate the assumptions undergirding each position. As the following discussion illustrates, such an outcome is the result of the very different and, at times, conflicting principles upon which each position is grounded.

Cultural relativism, as a concept for scholarly consideration, emerged in the discipline of anthropology in the former part of the twentieth century, although it has since become a mainstay in both social theory and empirical social research. Cultural relativism is predicated on the principle of 'difference' (Brems, 1997). Such a position contends that the idea of difference in culture engenders meaningful variation in terms of patterns of social relating and moral judgements. As such, proponents of this perspective assert that, '[a]lthough for every culture some moral judgements are valid, no moral judgement is universally valid. Every moral judgement is culturally relative' (Tilley, 2000, p. 505). This culturally-deterministic position advocates for not making moral judgements on the practices of the Other (Spiro, 1986), as such judgements necessarily emerges from one's own cultural— which is, of course, value-laden—reference points. As proponents of this view believe that cultural particularlism ought to be respected, no credence is afforded to, for instance, the conventional idea of 'human rights' as such a concept applies to all persons regardless of cultural context.

Universalism is foregrounded in philosophies—dating back to the stoics, though appearing in its most prominent incarnation in modern liberalism— that are predicated on the idea that certain rights ought to have universal applicability. Such a position 'holds that there is an underlying human unity which entitles all individuals, regardless of cultural or regional antecedents, to certain basic minimal rights' (Zechenter, 1997, p. 320). Within the juridical purview constructed by proponents of universalism, cultural particularlism does not offer a justifiable defense for contravening certain rights that are believed to be inalienable and, thus, available to all persons. That is to say, human rights trump the validity of those cultural practices that may violate the actualization of such rights. As the principle of universalism extends certain rights to all persons, without accounting for cultural situatedness, it has logically become the cornerstone in making the case for universal human rights, and in the enactment and the enforcement of human rights law (Donnelly, 2013; Morsink, 1999).

Given their diametrically opposing assumptions, each position vehemently repudiates the legitimacy of the other. On the one hand, cultural relativists accuse universalists of constructing a perverted version of *universal* human rights that reflects the interests of the hegemonic West (Brems, 1997). On the other hand, universalists accuse cultural relativists of providing a protective veil that thwarts criticism against those violent *cultural* practices that disproportionately harm the 'other' woman (Zechenter, 1997). In this chapter, we invoke Haraway's ideas by way to enter this bifurcated debate; in doing so, we illuminate how future research related to the experiences of the 'other' woman might be informed in the field of organization and management studies.

Feminist objectivity, situated knowledges, and the partial perspective

In the autumn of 1988, Haraway published her article, 'Situated knowledges,' in the journal *Feminist Studies*. In at least one important regard, this article may be read as a logical extension of her other landmark work from the period, 'A manifesto for cyborgs' (1985). Indeed, in 'A manifesto for cyborgs,' she offered the cyborg as an imaginative construct that subverts myriad ideological dichotomies, which function in the subjugation of women and other culturally disenfranchised subjects. For Haraway, the cyborg achieves its aim as 'it is chimera residing in indeterminate liminality—the corollary of confounded ontological demarcations that rigidly separate human, animal and machine, and that categorically differentiates the physical and non-physical constituents of (social and material) life' (Prasad, 2016a, p. 433). While foregrounding her argument in many of the same discourses which she engaged with in her earlier article, in 'Situated knowledges' Haraway negates the explicit notion of the cyborg though retains its ideational and political ethos by critically appraising the concept of 'objectivity' and, therein, developing a case for the 'partial perspective.'

Haraway commences her argument by revisiting how feminists, up until that point, have understood the idea of 'objectivity.' She explains that feminists read the concept in one of two antithetical ways. The first reading, and certainly the more popular one, is embedded in the position that all knowledge is socially circumscribed and, therefore, any claim to objectivity is wholly problematic if not entirely erroneous. The second reading, appearing in the tradition of humanistic Marxism and feminist empiricism, makes recourse to objectivity as an incidental byproduct of a disavowal of the anti-realist position that there exists no structure or materiality beyond that which is socially constructed. Taking her analytical departure from these bifurcated positions on objectivity, Haraway enquires,

> how [do we] have *simultaneously* an account of radical historical contingency for all knowledge claims and knowing subjects, a critical practice for recognizing our own "semiotic technologies" for making meanings, *and* a no-nonsense commitment to faithful accounts of a "real" world.
>
> (p. 579, *emphasis* in original)

From this question, she develops her concept of feminist objectivity

In an endeavor to articulate the case for feminist objectivity, Haraway makes an appeal to 'vision.' She prefaces her definition of vision with an unequivocal repudiation of the disembodied form of vision that figures ubiquitously in Cartesian reasoning. Indeed, in Cartesian formulations, vision:

> [I]s the gaze that mythically inscribes all the marked bodies, that makes the unmarked category claim the power to see and not be seen, to represent while escaping representation. This gaze signifies the unmarked positions of Man and White, one of the many nasty tones of "objectivity" to feminist ears.
>
> (p. 581)

Instead, Haraway calls for an embodied and a grounded understanding of vision. Such a reconfiguration, which would render vision to be an embodied and grounded sensory system, allows for the reclaiming of objectivity; that is, 'objectivity turns out to be about the particular and specific embodiment and definitely not about false vision promising transcendence of all limits and responsibilities' (pp. 582–583). Haraway crystallizes her position on the concept by elucidating that:

> Feminist objectivity is about limited location and situated knowledge, not about transcendence and splitting subject and object. It allows us to become answerable ... [indeed, her] essay is an argument for situated and embodied knowledges and an argument against various forms of unlocatable, and so irresponsible, knowledge claims.
>
> (p. 583)

Thus, feminist objectivity provides conceptual space from which to engage in discourses pertaining to the material conditions of disenfranchised subjects without succumbing to the seductive temptation of rendering truth-claims that profess their own universal relevance and ideological neutrality. Indeed, as Haraway remarks, '[f]eminist objectivity means quite simply *situated knowledges*' (p. 581, *emphasis* in original).

For the purposes of this chapter, it is important to emphasize how Haraway's concepts of feminist objectivity, situated knowledges, and the partial perspective, intervene in the debate over universalism versus relativism. Haraway is suspicious of both extremities of the debate. Indeed, she understands that both universalism and relativism relegate women and perform in the disservice of the project for gender egalitarianism; although she is equally cognizant of the very different rhetorical mechanisms that are deployed by each position to attempt to insulate itself from critique. Haraway deconstructs both positions by identifying the gendered ontological locations from where arguments offered by adherents of universalism and relativism emerge.

Haraway is overtly leery of universalism. Her wariness of universalism can be attributed, at least in part, to many of the arguments that had been cited in feminist critiques of the concept that preceded her article. For Haraway, though, her primary concern is with how universalism has its ontological location at the disembodied site of 'being nowhere while claiming to see comprehensively' (p. 584). For claims emerging from this site to be afforded credence requires a yielding to the assumption of metaphysical duality. Haraway foresees how emergent claims from such a de-contextualized location can pose problematic consequences for members of marginalized groups. Indeed, as its claims are bereft of cultural contextualization, she argues that universality is 'irresponsible' inasmuch as it is 'unable to be

called into account' (p. 583). Haraway understands that because the location of universalism asserts its own disembodiment by its tautological attes-
tation of not residing within the authoritative province of any particular
subject(s)—and, so, the location cannot be directly linked to the ideological
interests of any subject(s)—any knowledge claims made from such a location ought to be considered irresponsible.

While being skeptical of universality, Haraway does not credulously
accept unqualified forms of relativism—a tendency, either unintentional or
purposeful, that is often found in the works of scholars who develop arguments criticizing universality. Namely, Haraway avoids romanticizing lived
realities of the 'other' woman by either uncritically or passively accepting
harmful practices inflicted upon her. Indeed, paralleling the logic of universality, she shows how relativism is based on the disembodied ontological location of 'being nowhere while claiming to be everywhere equally' (p.
584). Such a critical assessment of the location from where cultural relativism makes its knowledge claims is necessary to allow for any sort of calling
into 'account' those cultural practices (e.g., female genital mutilation, female
infanticide, widow sacrifice, acid violence) that levy harm onto the 'other'
woman's body. Equally as noteworthy, it is only the subversion of relativism
that would create space for discourse from where to make value-laden issu-
ances on such cultural practices. In her argument casting doubt on the merits
of relativism, Haraway does caution against the risk of (mis)appropriating
the 'other' woman's experiences by attempting to *speak for* them. To avert
such an outcome, she advocates for, what she terms, mobile positioning and
passionate detachment. Mobile positioning and passionate detachment con-
ceptualizes knowledge as partial and locatable and, within this scope, cultural
practices are to be accountable. It may be read that Spivak echoed such ideas
in her text, 'Can the subaltern speak?' (1988). Indeed, in the classic work,
Spivak demonstrates how the body of the self-immolated sati (sacrificed
widow) was rendered silent in the masculinist discourse propagated by—and
between—White colonizing men and elite indigenous men.

In sum, for Haraway, universalism and relativism 'are both "god tricks"
promising vision from everywhere and nowhere equally and fully' (p. 584)
and, through their prestidigitation, they perform in maintaining asymmetrical
power relations by functioning in the service of the powerful while, concomitantly, disenfranchising the disempowered. In positing this point within the
framework of the political project of (1980s) feminism, this would mean, of
course, serving men while disenfranchising women. Haraway deconstructs
the logic underlying universalism and relativism by stating that:

> I am arguing for politics and epistemologies of location, positioning,
> and situating, where partiality and not universality is the condition of

being heard to make rational knowledge claims. There are claims on people's lives. I am arguing for the view from a body, always a complex, contradictory, structuring, and structured body, versus the view from above, from nowhere, from simplicity.

(p. 589)

Insofar as Haraway suggests the paramountcy of the corporeal when accounting for knowledge and experience, her feminist project shares political affinity with postcolonial thought, which we consider in the following section.

The study of the 'other' woman in organization and management studies

To account for how the experiences of 'other' women have been studied thus far in organization and management studies, we would be remiss not to begin the discussion with some consideration of how the field has engaged with postcolonial theory. Postcolonial theory 'represents an attempt to investigate the complex and deeply fraught dynamics of Western colonialism and anticolonial resistance, and the ongoing significance of the colonial encounter for people's lives in the West and the non-West' (Prasad, 2003, p. 5; Jack, Westwood, Srinivas, & Sardar, 2011). It is particularly attendant to unravelling and problematizing the cultural dynamics that manifest at the liminal sites at which the experiences of the colonized and the colonizers converge.

In the last decade, critical management scholars have used postcolonial theory to capture the cultural dynamics of a diverse range of organizational phenomena. For example, Westwood (2006), Özkazanç-Pan (2008), and Frenkel (2008) have each demonstrated how the analytical resources imparted by postcolonial theoretical frameworks can effectually critique (and re-imagine) some of the most fundamental ideas in the field—including, especially, those sites of study marked by overt liminality, such as international business and the multinational corporation. Other researchers in the field have applied postcolonial theory to empirical studies at different locations; therein, deciphering aspects of the situated lived realities of geographically disparate subjects sharing only the commonality of being impacted by the colonial experience. In this vein, Ulus (2015) and Dar (2017) employ postcolonial theory to elucidate the interpersonal dynamics of workplace emotions, and the hegemony of the English language over indigenous languages in NGOs, respectively, in contemporary India. Nkomo (2011) adopts a postcolonial lens to critically appraise the problematic ways in which African leaders and African management have been represented. Prasad (2014) uses postcolonial theory to deconstruct the psychoanalytic dynamics of fieldwork conducted in the Occupied Palestinian Territories.

While it has certainly benefited organizational analysis generally, the analytical site at which postcolonial theory has been particularly useful in relation to the complex experiences of 'other' women is that where feminist theorizing and feminist practice intersect. Indeed, several authors in organization and management studies have developed their arguments at the interface at which postcolonial theory meets feminism. Banu Özkazanç-Pan (2019) draws on a postcolonial feminist framework to identify the gendered dimensions of corporate social responsibility (CSR) efforts in the global South. Analyzing the case of the Rana Plaza disaster in Bangladesh and, more importantly, the institutionalized changes that followed in its aftermath—which, at least overtly, sought to better the working conditions of those subjects most harmed by the disaster (i.e., disenfranchised local women working in garment manufacturing)— Özkazanç-Pan reads the neocolonial discourses that emerge when Western-based corporations pursue CSR projects in the Global South. She concludes that among the (unintended) effects, 'CSR imbues the specter of rights on its gendered subaltern subjects without affording agency, thereby (re)constructing neocolonial relations in the context of globalized neoliberalism and capitalism.'

Whereas Özkazanç-Pan (2019) identifies the palpable neocolonial discourses that are reinscribed discursively in a contemporary manifestation of south/north capitalist arrangements, Jennifer Manning (2018) has extended the discussion by suggesting trajectories through which researchers in the field could pursue decolonial feminist ethnography. Drawing on her own experiences in conducting ethnographic fieldwork with Maya women in Guatemala, Manning concludes:

[D]ecolonial feminist theory challenges the coloniality of knowledge and gender to contribute to the decolonization of [organization and management studies] based on the experiences of world views of marginalized, indigenous, non-Westernized women to construct a new indigenous feminist geopolitics of knowledge and knowing.

(p. 314)

For her, coming from Western geographical spaces does not necessarily preclude a researcher from studying the experiences of the 'other' woman. However, to negate the issues raised in the criticism of Mohanty and Spivak—which we cited at the introduction of this chapter—Manning implores researchers to meaningfully consider questions of *positionality* and *representation*. Positionality acknowledges the salient differences that exist in terms of position, privilege, and power between the scholar and the 'other' woman. Representation calls for resisting the temptation to assume that the 'other' woman is either voiceless or that they do not know what is in their best interests and, therefore, the researcher must assume the role of knowledge authority by seeking to (re)present their voice. Positionality and representation underscore further the point that it is critical to *speak with* rather than *speak for* the 'other' woman with whom the researcher is engaging. Adopting Manning's recommendations would effectively bring the 'other' 'woman's lives to the forefront and [construct] situated knowledge to provide missing perspectives' (Jain, 2017, p. 569).

Synthesizing the objections raised by Özkazanç-Pan and Manning—and those offered earlier by critical management scholars who have previously adopted postcolonial thought—reveals the potential of Haraway's conceptual insights for the field of organization and management studies. Indeed, these scholars oppose the forms of knowledge construction that are unitary and claim their own disembodied objectivity; thereby, relegating the 'other' woman's modes of knowing. It is in conceptually substantiating the opposition of this perspective that Haraway's ideas are critical. More specifically, feminist objectivity, situated knowledges, and the partial perspective perform to understand cultural differences, yet not essentialize such differences in ways that would problematically suspend discourse on the marginal experiences of women across and within cultures—regardless of whether or not they are qualified as 'other.'

To elaborate on the point of how Haraway's concepts prevent the closure of certain discourses pertaining, especially, to 'other' women's experiences, it is useful to return to Lila Abu-Lughod's thought-provoking article, 'Do Muslim women really need saving?' (2002). In critiquing the debate over the burqa, which effectively offered certain ideological grounds—which were, of course, couched as a moral imperative—for military action against Afghanistan in the aftermath of 9/11, Abu-Lughod nuances the bifurcated debate between universalism and relativism. As she writes:

> [W]hen I talk about accepting difference, I am not implying that we should resign ourselves to being cultural relativists who respect whatever goes on elsewhere as "just their culture" … [there are] dangers of "cultural" explanations; "their" cultures are just as much part of history and an interconnected world as ours are. What I am advocating is the hard work involved in recognizing and respecting differences— precisely as products of different histories, as expressions of different circumstances, and as manifestations of differently structured desires. We may want justice for women, but can we accept that there might be

different ideas about justice and that different women might want, or choose, different futures from what we envision as best?

(pp. 787–788)

For Abu-Lughod, if cultural differences are to be appreciated constructively—that is to say, in a way that does not automatically subscribe to the extreme version of cultural relativism—it is crucial, returning to Haraway's vernacular, to assume a partial perspective that would allow for the emergence of situated knowledges through an engagement with feminist objectivity.

In sum, while several critical management scholars have observed the need to reject the overt—or, as it is more likely the case, the tacit—ethnocentricism undergirding research in the field (Frenkel, 2008; Özkazanç-Pan, 2008; Prasad, 2016b; Westwood, 2006), few conceptual and analytical tools have been offered by which to realize this outcome. Haraway provides the conceptual and analytical tools necessary by which to disavow the (unintentional) ethnocentricism that detrimentally affects—or minimally, negates—the life of the 'other' woman during the research process. While making possible the extrication of ethnocentricism during the research process, Haraway's ideas, concurrently, allow for *critical* engagements with the 'other' woman's experiences—and this means, above all, sensitivity towards the *situated knowledges* of these 'other' women through the adoption of a *partial perspective*.

Concluding remarks

While there are a few examples of Haraway's ideas being incorporated in meaningful ways into research in organization and management studies (e.g., Bowring, 2004; Durepos, Prasad, & Villaneuva, 2016; Muhr, 2011; Muhr & Rehn, 2015; Prasad, 2016a), in a review of feminist theory in the field, Harding, Ford, and Fotaki (2013) underscored that the full potential of Haraway's works remains underutilized. In this chapter, we have moved towards responding to this oversight by identifying how Haraway's concepts of feminist objectivity, situated knowledges, and the partial perspective can constructively inform future research on various social—and, specifically, organizational—phenomena. This broadens the work completed elsewhere by two of the authors of this chapter who cite Haraway's ideas for their ability to subvert the problematic notion that *a priori* conditions govern the theorizing process (Segarra & Prasad, 2018). Such an assumption underlying theorizing—and knowledge construction, more generally—of course disproportionately harms women by de-legitimating their experiences and their modes of knowing (Hopfl, 2000; Phillips, Pullen, & Rhodes, 2014).

With the overall intention of advancing feminist organization studies, this chapter illustrates how the conceptual ideas proffered by Haraway can explore the possibilities that would emerge when the bifurcated and politically untenable positions of universality and relativism are deconstructed.

Recommended reading

Original text by Donna Haraway

Haraway, D. (1991). *Simians, Cyborgs, and Women: The Reinvention of Nature*. New York: Routledge.

Key academic text

Penley, C., Ross, A. and Haraway, D. (1990). Cyborgs at large: Interview with Donna Haraway. *Social Text*, 25/26, 8–23.

Accessible resource

Prasad, A. (2016). Cyborg writing as a political act: Reading Donna Haraway in organization studies. *Gender, Work and Organization*, 23(4), 431–446.

References

Abu-Lughod, L. (2002). Do Muslim women really need saving? Anthropological reflections on cultural relativism and its others. *American Anthropologist*, 104(3), 783–790.

Bowring, M. (2004). Resistance is not futile: Liberating Captain Janeway from the masculine-feminine dualism of leadership. *Gender, Work and Organization*, 11(4), 381–405.

Brems, E. (1997). Enemies or allies? Feminism or cultural relativism as dissident voices in human rights discourse. *Human Rights Quarterly*, 19(1), 136–164.

Dar, S. (2017). De-colonizing the boundary-object. *Organization Studies*, 39(4), 565–584.

Dembour, M.-B. (2001). Following the movement of a pendulum: Between universalism and relativism. In: J. K. Cowan, M.-B. Dembour, & R. A. Wilson (Eds), *Culture and Rights: Anthropological Perspectives* (pp. 56–79). Cambridge: Cambridge University Press.

Donnelly, J. (2013). *Universal Human Rights in Theory and Practice* (3rd ed.). Ithaca: Cornell University Press.

Durepos, G., Prasad, A., & Villanueva, C. E. (2016). How might we study international business to account for marginalized subjects? Turning to practice and situating knowledges. *Critical Perspectives on International Business*, 12(3), 306–314.

Frenkel, M. (2008). The multinational corporation as a third space: Rethinking international management discourse on knowledge transfer through Homi Bhabha. *Academy of Management Review*, 33(4), 924–942.

Haraway, D. (1985). A manifesto for cyborgs: Science, technology and socialist feminism in the 1980s. *Socialist Review*, 80, 65–107.

Haraway, D. (1988). Situated knowledges: The science question in feminism and the privilege of partial perspective. *Feminist Studies*, 14(3), 575–599.

Harding, N., Ford, J., & Fotaki, M. (2013). Is the 'F'-word still dirty? A past, present and future of/for feminist and gender studies in *Organization*. *Organization*, 20(1), 51–65.

Höpfl, H. (2000). The suffering mother and the miserable son: Organizing women and women's writing. *Gender, Work and Organization*, 7(2), 98–105.

Jack, G., Westwood, R., Srinivas, N., & Sardar, Z. (2011). Deepening, broadening and re-asserting a postcolonial interrogative space in organization studies. *Organization*, 18(3), 275–302.

Jain, T. (2017). Researcher vs advocate: Ethnographic-ethical dilemmas in feminist scholarship. *Equality, Diversity and Inclusion: An International Journal*, 36(6), 566–585.

Manning, J. (2018). Becoming a decolonial feminist ethnographer: Addressing the complexities of positionality and representation. *Management Learning*, 49(3), 311–326.

Mohanty, C. T. (1984). Under western eyes: Feminist scholarship and colonial discourses. *Boundary 2*, 12(3), 333–358.

Morsink, J. (1999). *The Universal Declaration of Human Rights: Origins, Drafting and Intent*. Philadelphia: University of Pennsylvania Press.

Muhr, S. L. (2011). Caught in the gendered machine: On the masculine and the feminine in cyborg leadership. *Gender, Work and Organization*, 18(3), 337–357.

Muhr, S. L., & Rehn, A. (2015). On gendered technologies and cyborg writing. *Gender, Work and Organization*, 22(2), 129–138.

Nkomo, S. M. (2011). A postcolonial and anti-colonial reading of 'African' leadership and management in organization studies: Tensions, contradictions and possibilities. *Organization*, 18(3), 365–386.

Özkazanç-Pan, B. (2008). International management research meets 'the rest of the world.' *Academy of Management Review*, 33(4), 964–974.

Özkazanç-Pan, B. (2019). CSR as gendered neocoloniality in the global south. *Journal of Business Ethics*, 160, 851–864. doi:10.1007/s10551-018-3798-1.

Phillips, M., Pullen, A., & Rhodes, C. (2014). Writing organization as a gendered practice: Interrupting the libidinal economy. *Organization Studies*, 35(3), 313–333.

Prasad, A. (2003). The gaze of the other: Postcolonial theory and organizational analysis. In: A. Prasad (Ed.), *Postcolonial Theory and Organizational Analysis: A Critical Engagement* (pp. 3–43). New York: Palgrave Macmillan.

Prasad, A. (2014). You can't go home again: And other psychoanalytic lessons from crossing a neo-colonial border. *Human Relations*, 67(2), 233–257.

Prasad, A. (2016a). Cyborg writing as a political act: Reading Donna Haraway in organization studies. *Gender, Work and Organization*, 23(4), 431–446.

Prasad, A. (2016b). The fact of otherness: Towards liberating the subaltern consciousness in contemporary management research. In: T. Beyes, M. Parker, & C. Steyaert (Eds.), *Routledge Companion to Reinventing Management Education* (pp. 454–467). New York: Routledge.

Said, E. W. (1978). *Orientalism*. New York: Pantheon Books.

Segarra, P., & Prasad, A. (2018). How does corporeality inform theorizing? Revisiting Hannah Arendt and the banality of evil. *Human Studies*, 41, 545–563. doi:10.1007/s10746-018-9474-8.

Spiro, M. E. (1986). Cultural relativism and the future of anthropology. *Cultural Anthropology*, 1(3), 259–286.

Spivak, G. C. (1988). Can the subaltern speak? In: C. Nelson & L. Grossberg (Eds.), *Marxism and the Interpretation of Culture* (pp. 271–313). Urbana: University of Illinois Press.

Tilley, J. J. (2000). Cultural relativism. *Human Rights Quarterly*, 22(2), 501–547.

Ulus, E. (2015). Workplace emotions in postcolonial spaces: Enduring legacies, ambivalence, and subversion. *Organization*, 22(6), 890–908.

Westwood, R. (2006). International business and management studies as an orientalist discourse: A postcolonial critique. *Critical Perspectives on International Business*, 2(2), 91–113.

Zechenter, E. M. (1997). In the name of culture: Cultural relativism and the abuse of the individual. *Journal of Anthropological Research*, 53(3), 319–347.

Index

Printed in the United States
by Baker & Taylor Publisher Services